THE Benny Goodman COLLECTION

Transcribed and adapted for piano solo by Forrest "Woody" Mankowski

ISBN 0-634-03536-3

HAL•LEONARD® CORPORATION

7777 W. BLUEMOUND RD. P.O. BOX 13819 MILWAUKEE, WI 53213

Visit Hal Leonard Online at
www.halleonard.com

DISCOGRAPHY

Air Mail Special – Charlie Christian: *The Genius of the Electric Guitar*; (Columbia CK 40846)

And the Angels Sing – Benny Goodman: *The Ultimate Collection*; (Prism PLATCD 448)

Avalon – *The Small Groups*; (Living Era CDAJA 5144)

Blue Skies – Benny Goodman: *The Ultimate Collection*; (Prism PLATCD 448)

Body and Soul – Ken Burns Jazz: *Benny Goodman*; (Columbia/Legacy 61445)

Clarinade – *Benny Goodman Plays Mel Powell*; (HEP CD 1055)

Darn That Dream – *Benny Goodman Plays Eddie Sauter*; (HEP CD 1053)

Don't Be That Way – Benny Goodman: *The Ultimate Collection*; (Prism PLATCD 448)

The Earl – *Benny Goodman Plays Mel Powell*; (HEP CD 1055)

Flying Home – *Benny Goodman Sextet*; (Columbia CK 45144)

Goodbye – Benny Goodman: *The Ultimate Collection*; (Prism PLATCD 448)

Gotta Be This or That – *Benny Goodman and His Great Vocalists*; (Columbia/Legacy CK 66198)

I'm Here – *Benny Goodman Plays Mel Powell*; (HEP CD 1055)

Jersey Bounce – *Benny Goodman Plays Mel Powell*; (HEP CD 1055)

King Porter Stomp – Benny Goodman: *The Ultimate Collection*; (Prism PLATCD 448)

Let's Dance – Benny Goodman: *The Ultimate Collection*; (Prism PLATCD 448)

Mission to Moscow – *Benny Goodman Plays Mel Powell*; (HEP CD 1055)

Moonglow – Benny Goodman: *The Ultimate Collection*; (Prism PLATCD 448)

More Than You Know – *Benny Goodman Plays Eddie Sauter*; (HEP CD 1053)

Seven Come Eleven – Charlie Christian: *The Genius of the Electric Guitar*; (Columbia CK 40846)

Sing, Sing, Sing – *Sing, Sing, Sing*; (Bluebird/RCA 5630)

A Smooth One – *Benny Goodman Sextet*; (Columbia CK 45144)

Sometimes I'm Happy – *Sing, Sing, Sing*; (Bluebird/RCA 5630)

Stealin' Apples – Benny Goodman: *The Ultimate Collection*; (Prism PLATCD 448)

Stompin' At the Savoy – Benny Goodman: *The Ultimate Collection*; (Prism PLATCD 448)

Sugar Foot Stomp – Benny Goodman: *The Ultimate Collection*; (Prism PLATCD 448)

This Year's Kisses – Billie Holiday: *This Is Jazz #15*; (Columbia/Legacy CK 64622)

Why Don't You Do Right – *Benny Goodman Plays Mel Powel*; (HEP CD 1055)

The World Is Waiting for the Sunrise – *The Small Groups*; (Living Era CDAJA 5144)

CONTENTS

AIR MAIL SPECIAL

By BENNY GOODMAN,
JIMMY MUNDY and CHARLIE CHRISTIAN

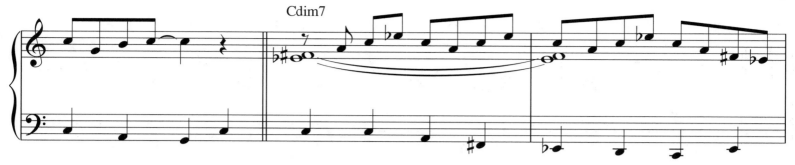

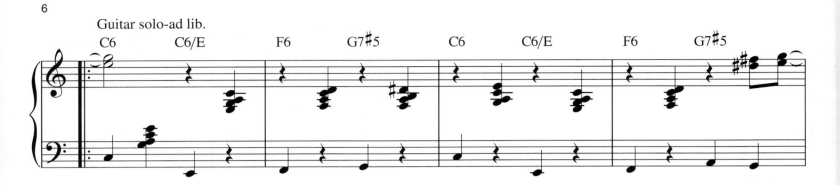

Guitar solo-ad lib.

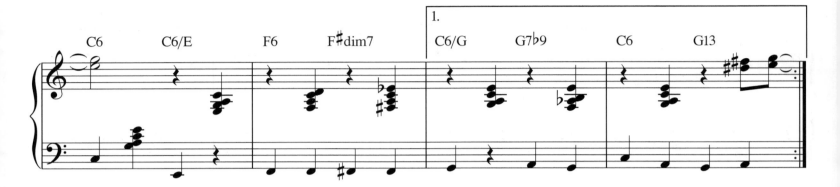

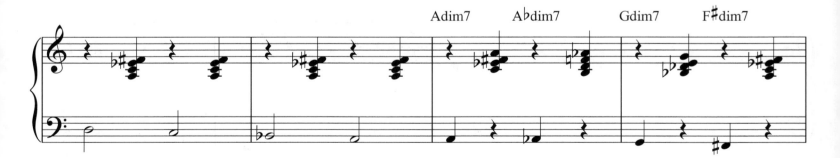

Benny Goodman clarinet solo:

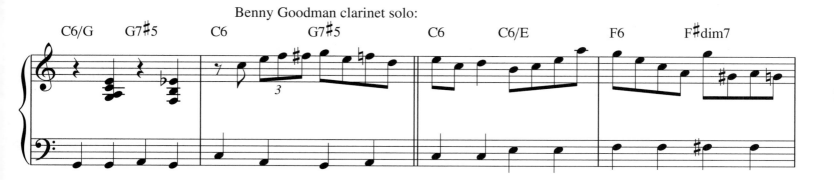

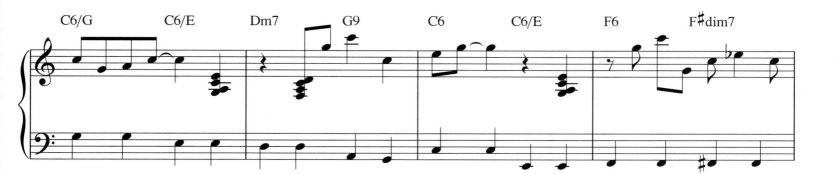

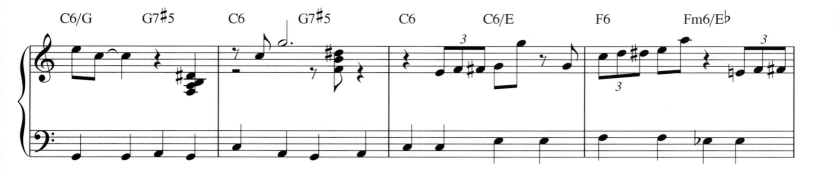

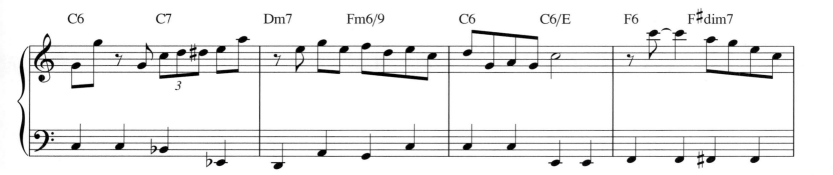

8

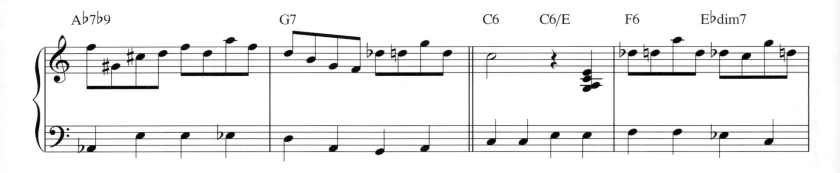

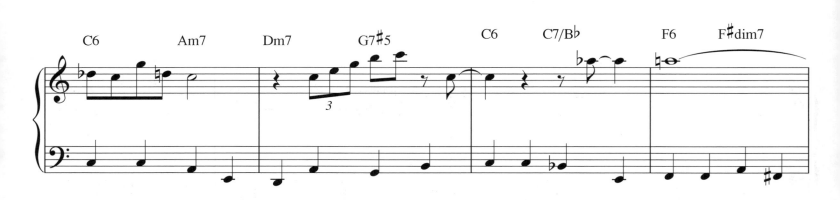

Trumpet solo-ad lib.

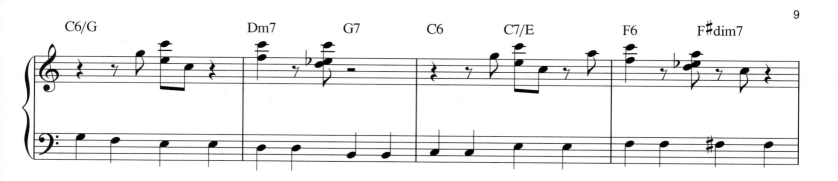

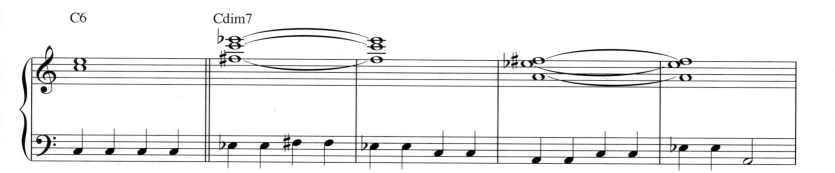
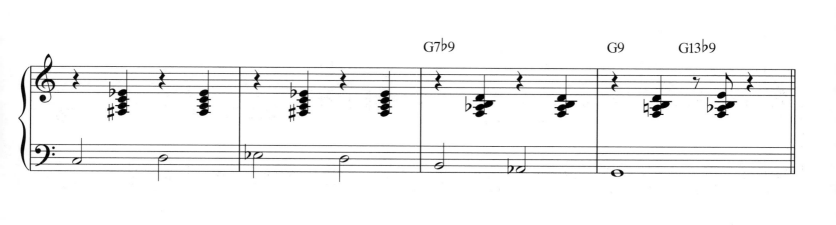
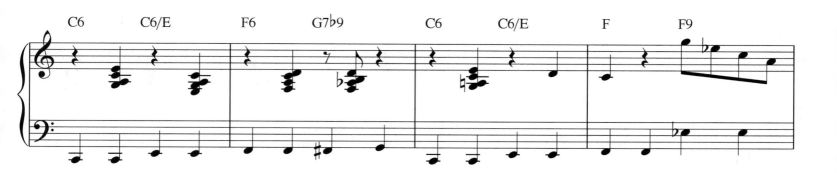

Saxophone solo-ad lib.

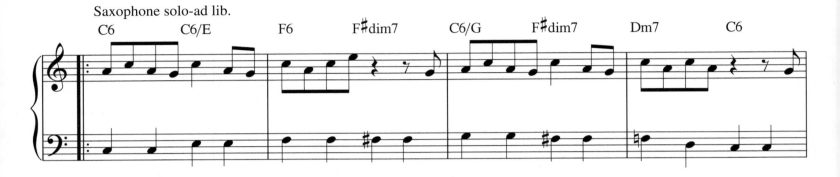

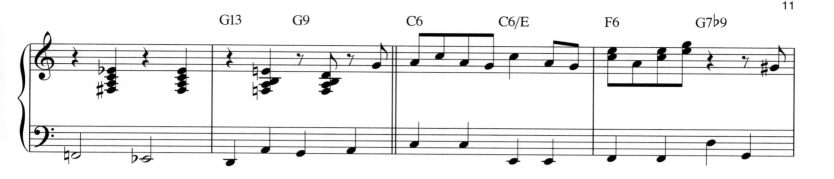

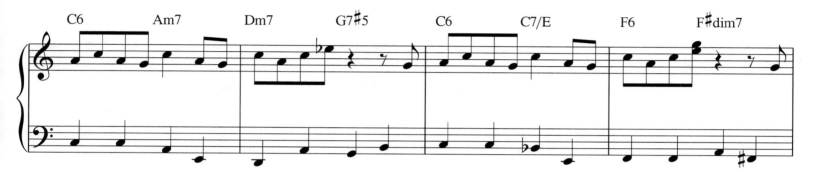

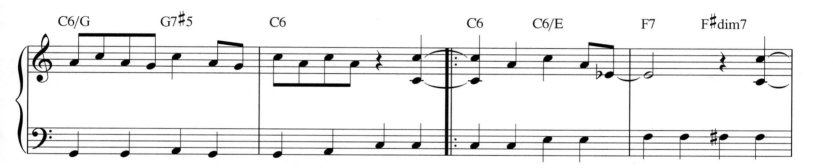

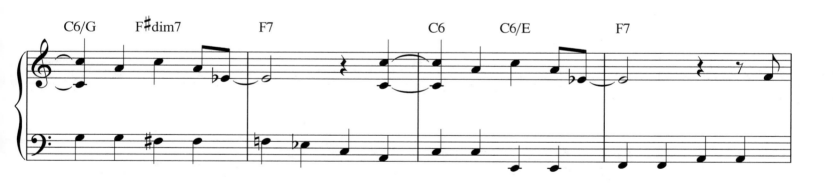

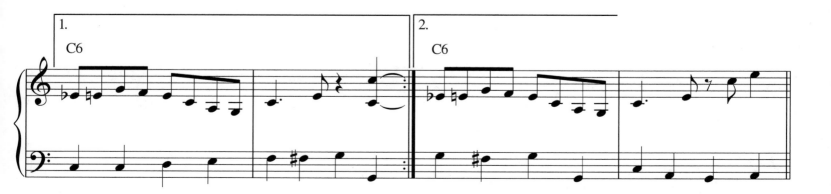

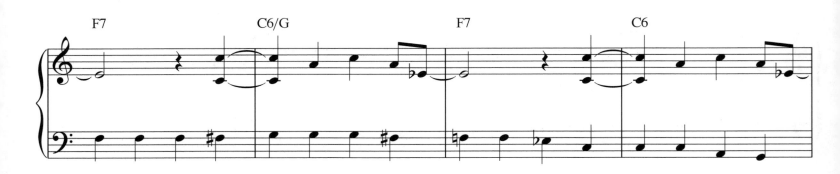

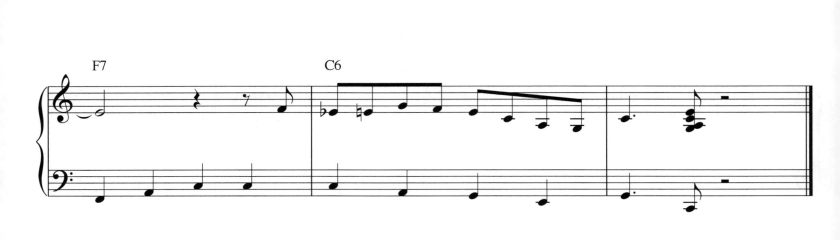

AVALON

Words by AL JOLSON and B.G. DeSYLVA
Music by VINCENT ROSE

Bright tempo

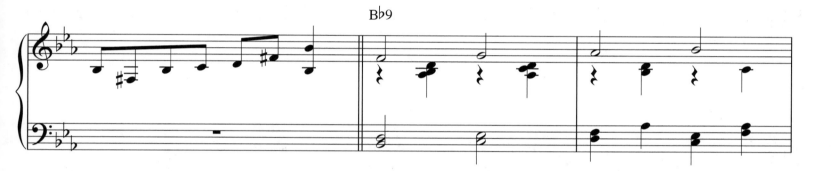

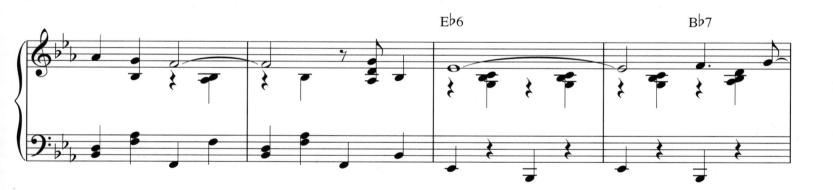

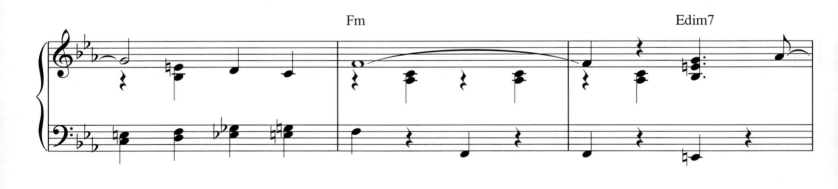

Piano solo:

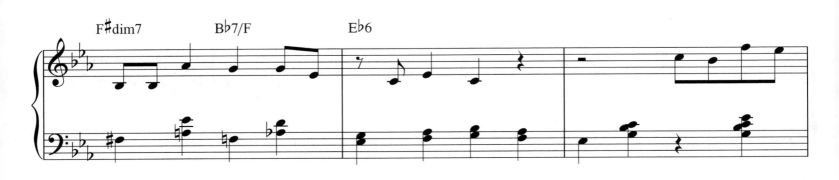

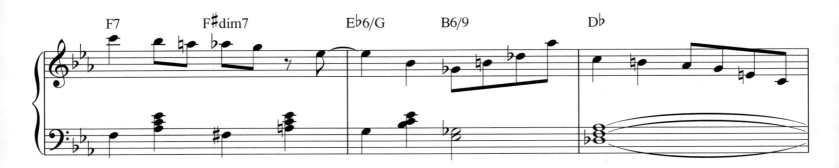

Benny Goodman clarinet solo:

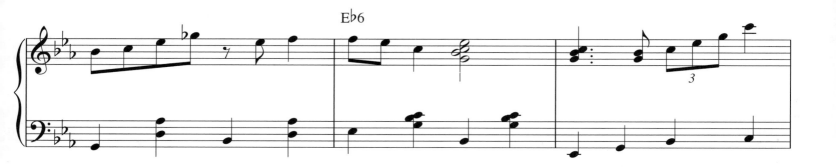

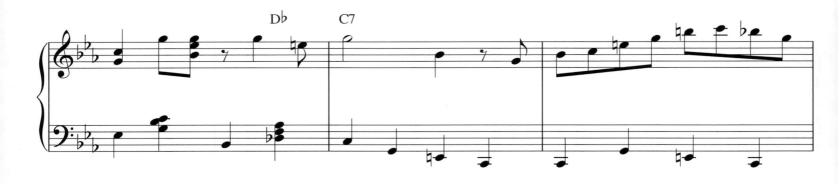

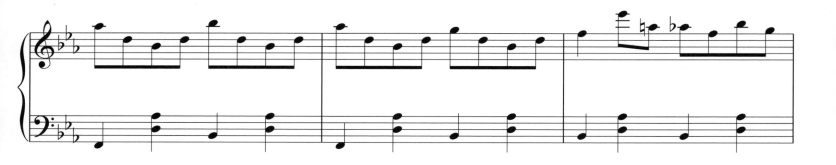

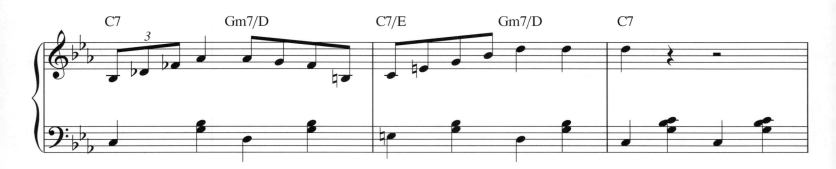

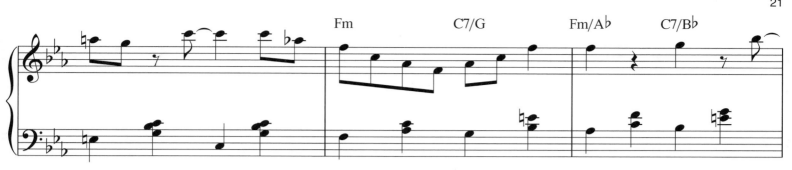

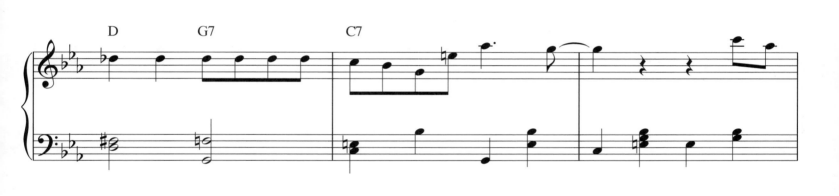

22

AND THE ANGELS SING

Music by ZIGGY ELMAN
Words by JOHNNY MERCER

Moderately slow Swing

We meet___ speak

and the an - gels sing,
and the an - gels sing.

___ the an - gels sing the sweet - est song ___
___ Or am I read - ing mu - sic in -

I ev - er heard.___   You
- to ev - ery word?___

Sud - den - ly, ___   the

set - ting is strange.___   I can see wa - ter and moon - light beam - ing, ___

sil - ver waves___ that break on some un - dis - cov - ered shore.

Bb9

Then sud - den - ly, ___ I see it all change,

Eb6   Cm7/F   F9

long win - ter nights with the can - dles gleam - ing. ___ Through it all, your

C9   F7b9   Bb6   Gb13   F13

face that I ___ a - dore. ___   You

Bb6   Cm7   Bb6/D   Eb6   Bb6

smile   and the an - gels sing, ___

and though it's just a gen - tle___ mur - mur at the start.___

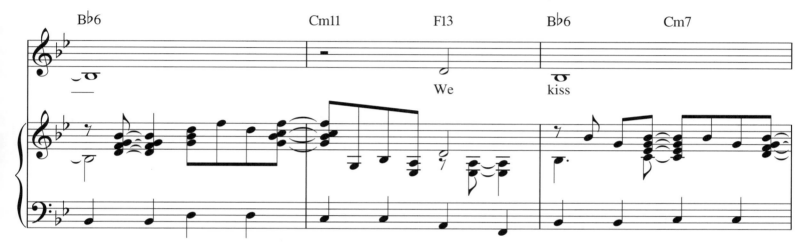

We kiss

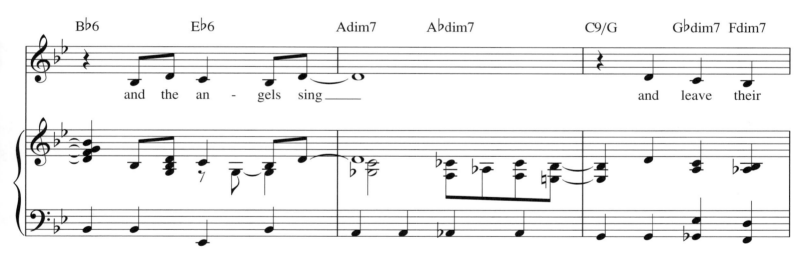

and the an - gels sing___ and leave their

mu - sic ring - ing in___ my heart._____

Faster (à la "Hava Nagila")

Drum solo:

Trumpet solo:

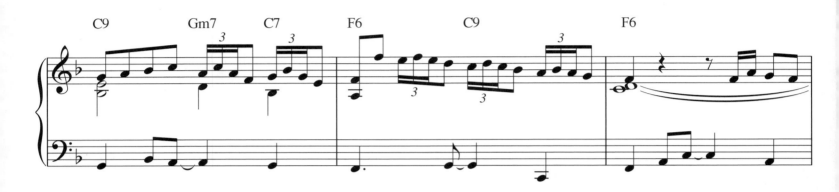

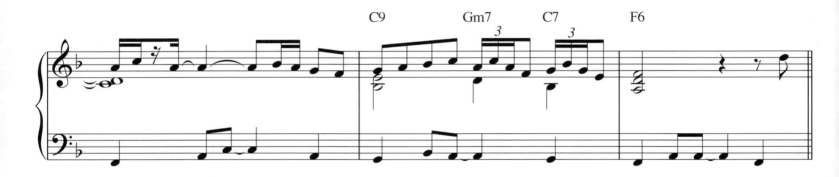

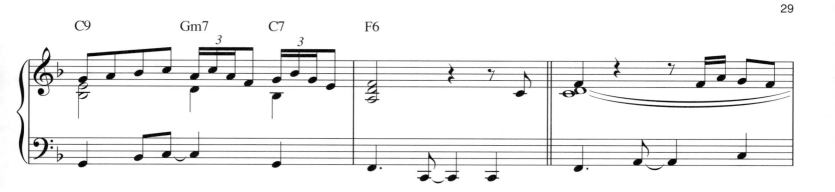

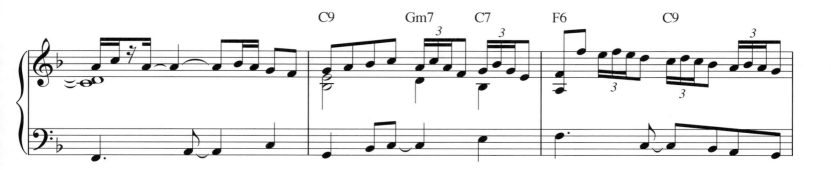

Slower (Tempo I)

30

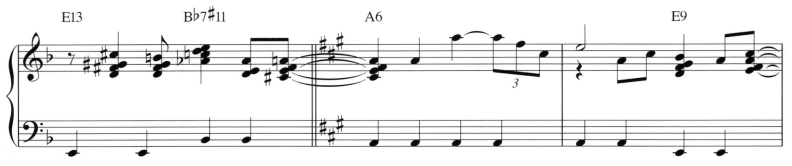

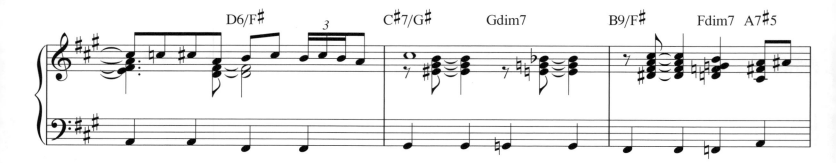

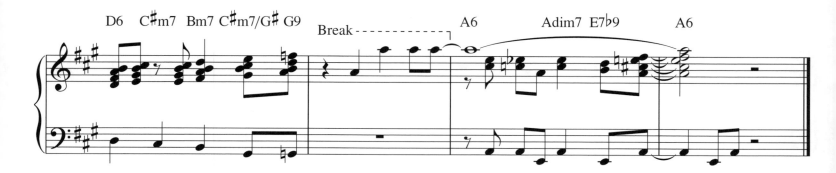

CLARINADE

By MEL POWELL

Bright Swing

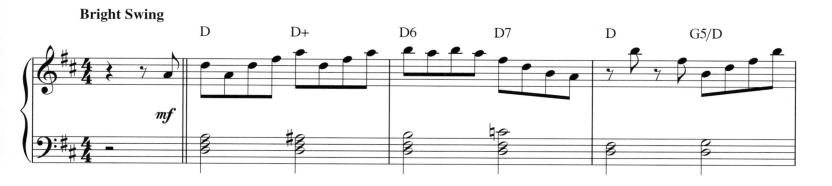

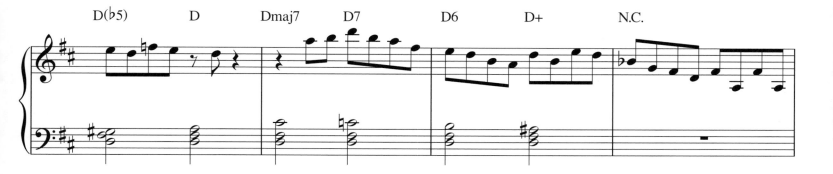

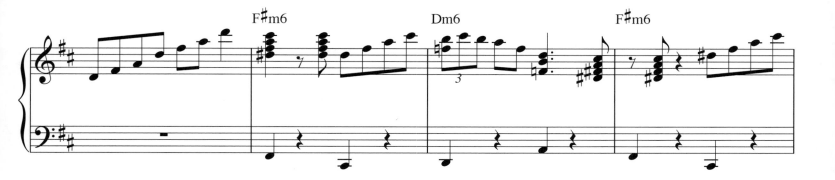

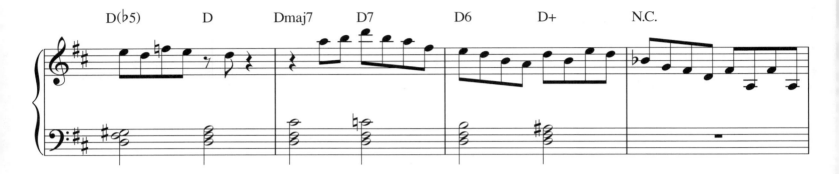

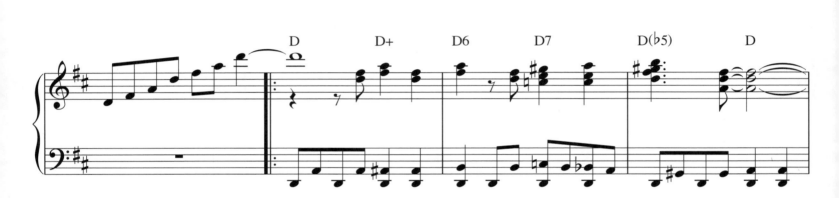

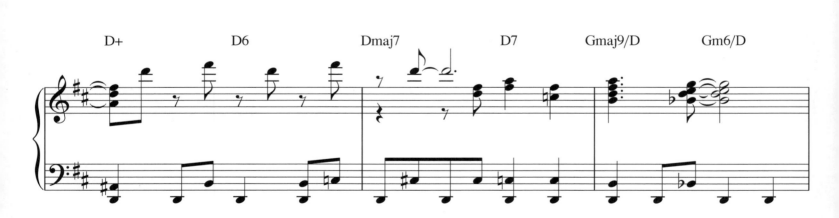

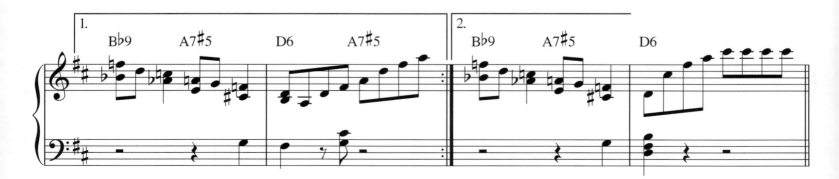

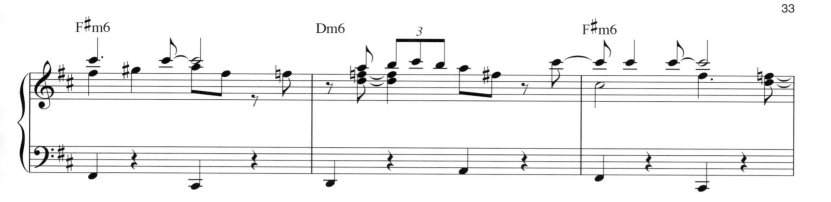

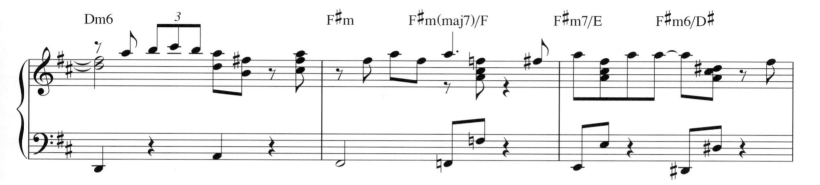

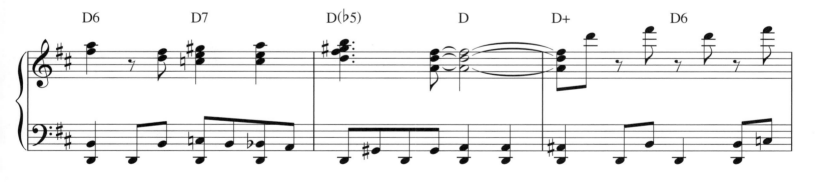

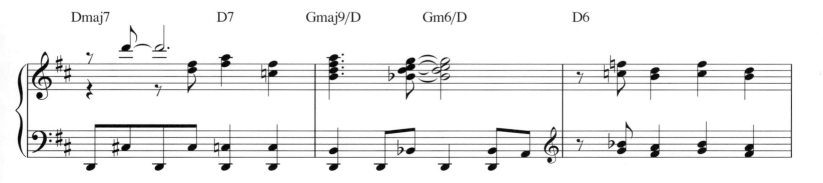

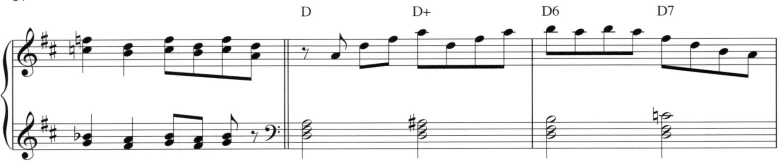

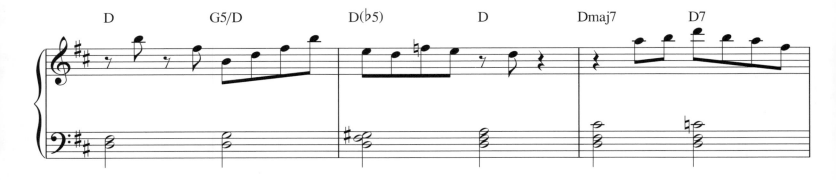

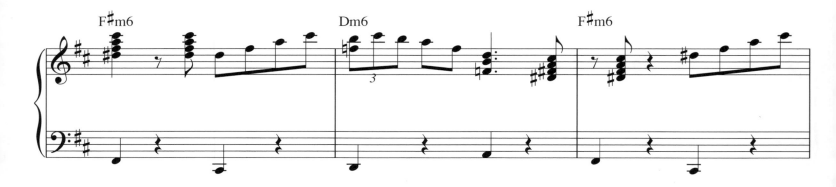

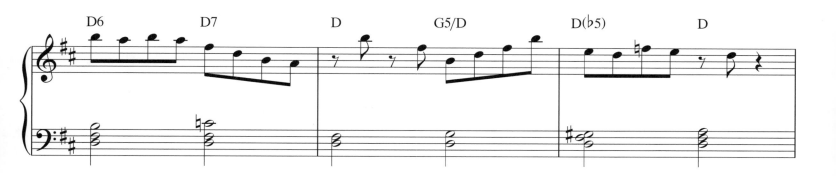

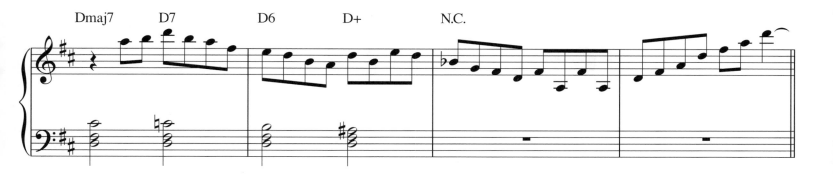

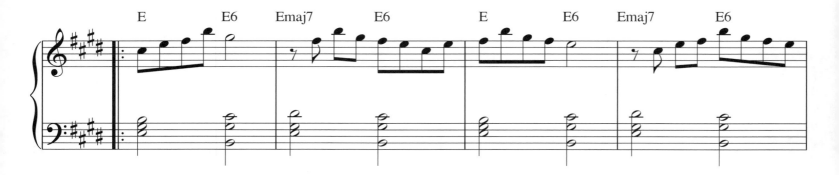

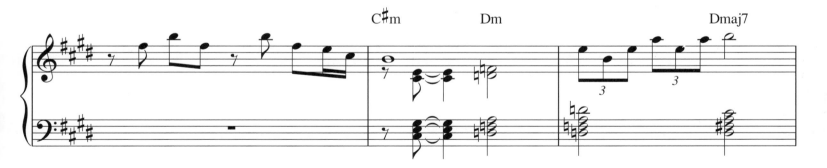

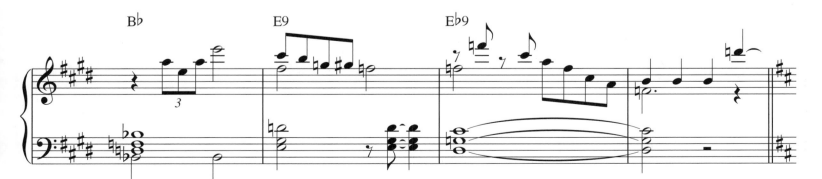

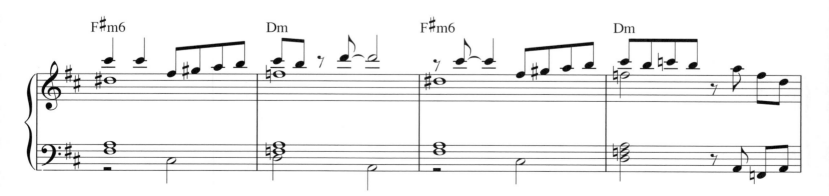

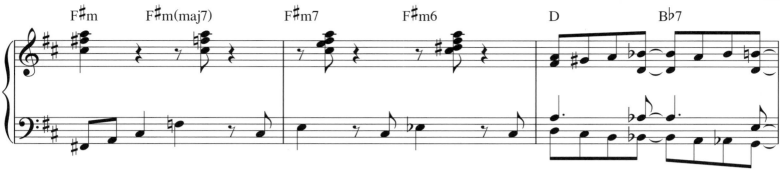

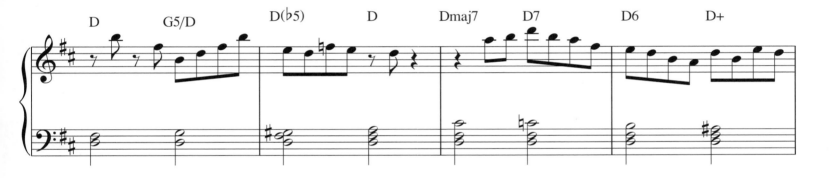

BLUE SKIES
from BETSY

Words and Music by
IRVING BERLIN

Moderate Dance tempo

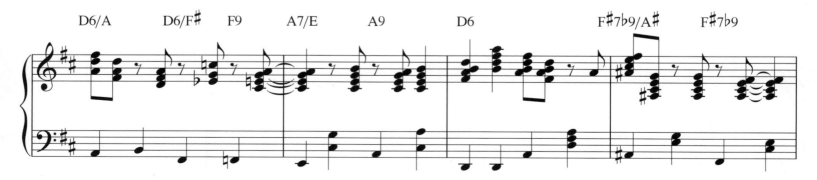

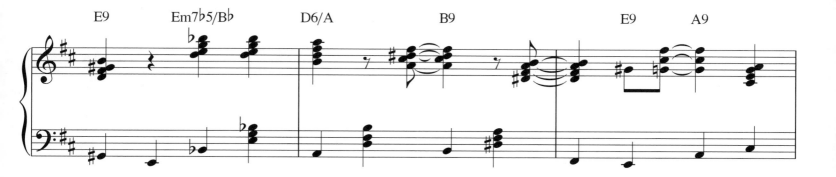

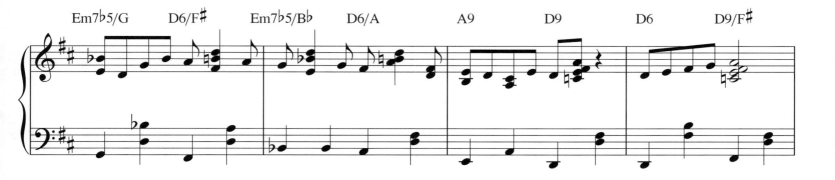

42

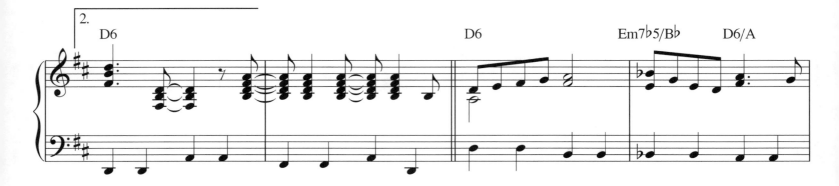

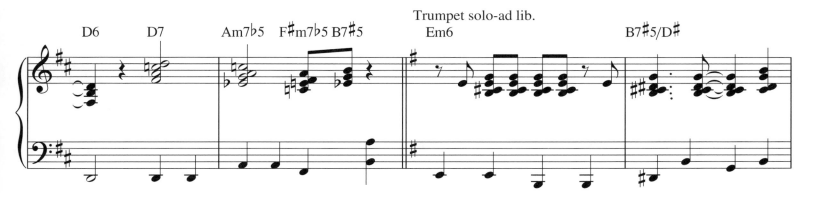

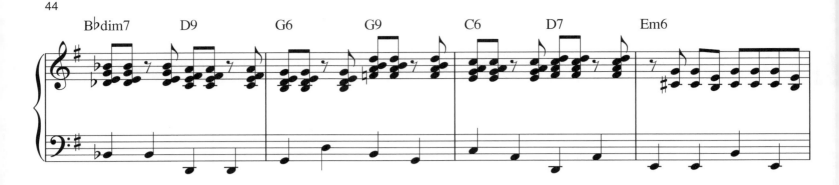

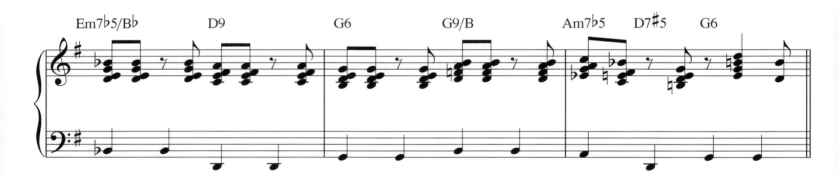

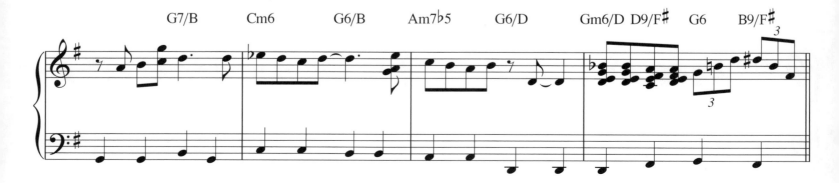

Benny Goodman clarinet solo:

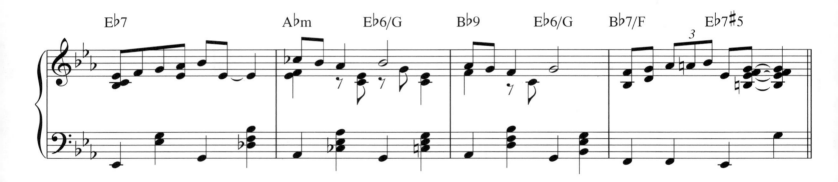

DON'T BE THAT WAY

By BENNY GOODMAN,
MITCHELL PARISH and EDGAR SAMPSON

Moderate Dance tempo

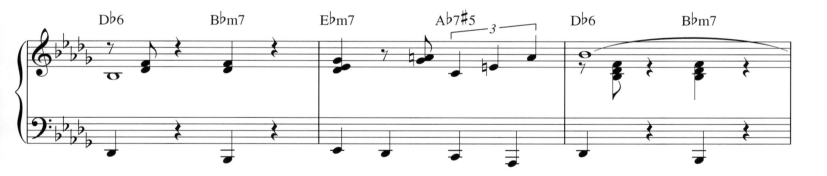

48

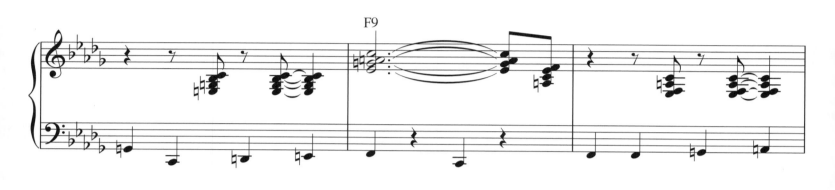

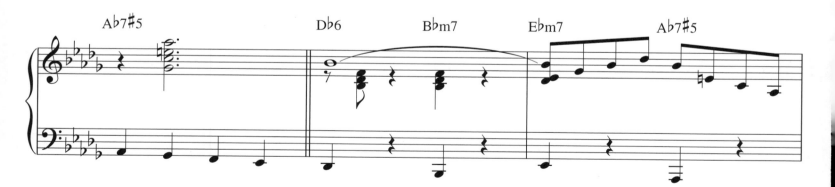

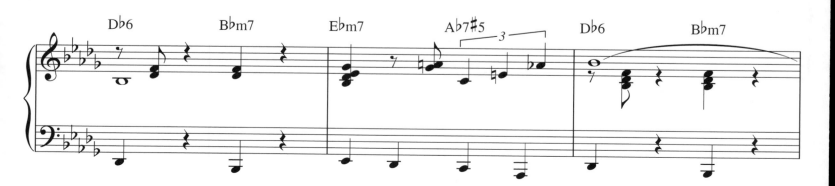

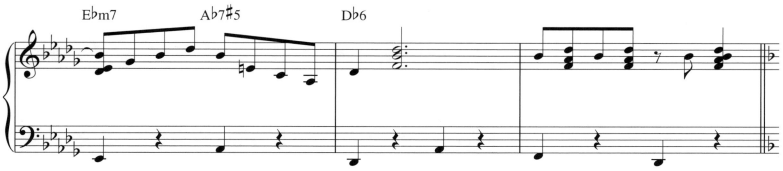

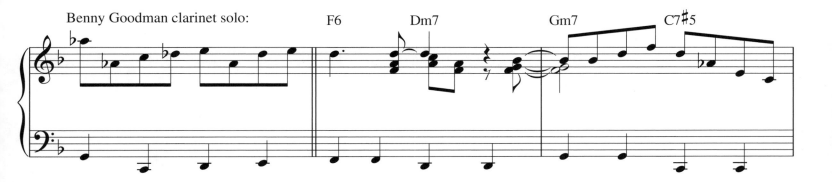

Benny Goodman clarinet solo:

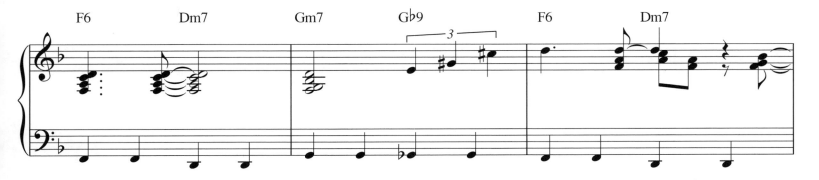

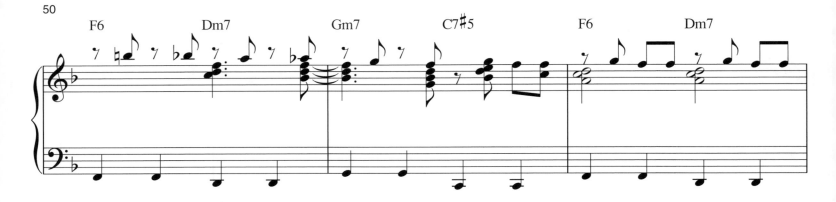

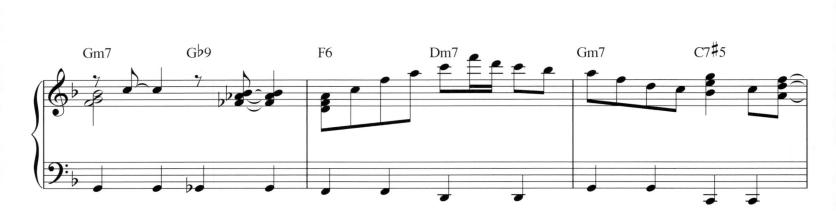

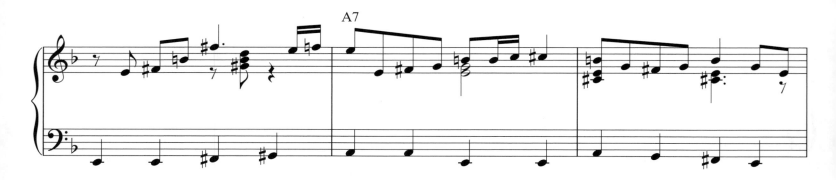

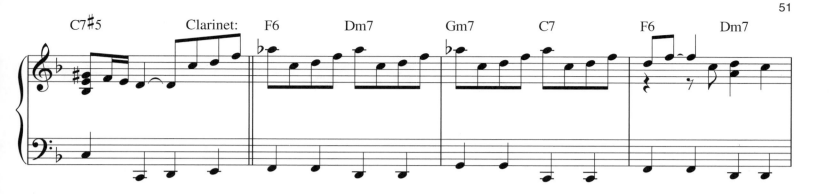

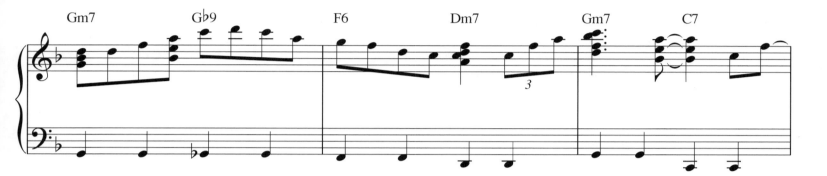

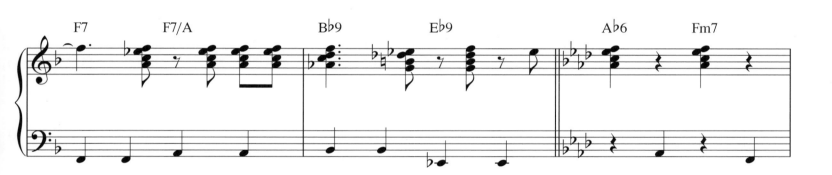

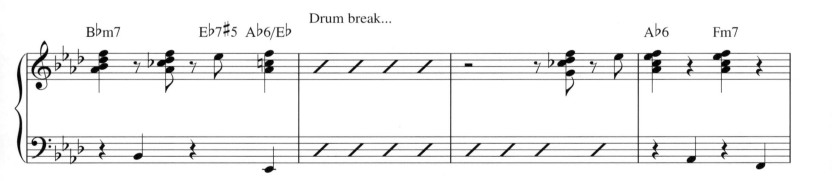

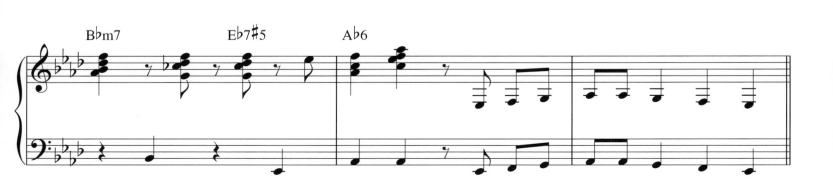

52

Trombone solo:

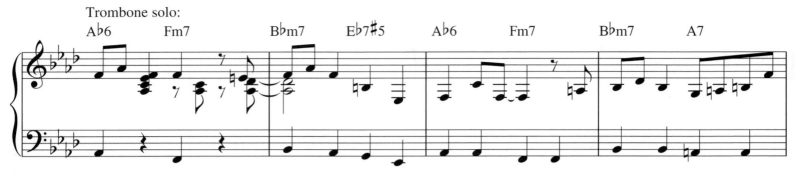

Play 4 times-decrescendo each time

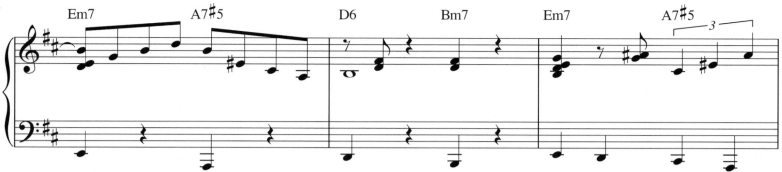

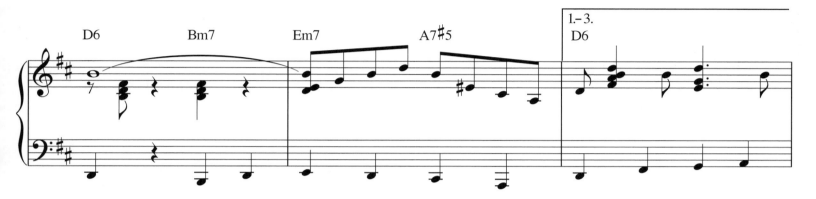

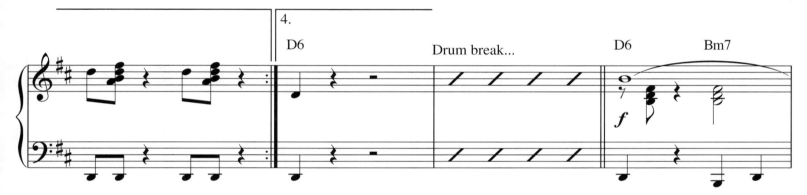

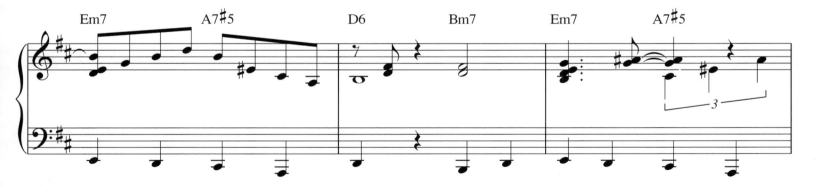

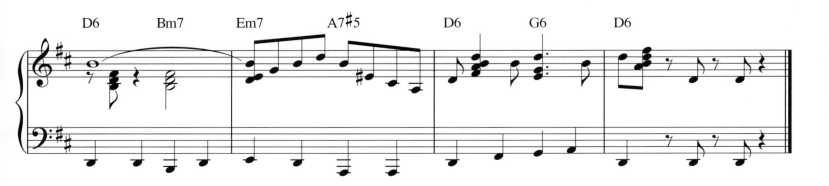

BODY AND SOUL

Words by EDWARD HEYMAN,
ROBERT SOUR and FRANK EYTON
Music by JOHN GREEN

Dance Ballad

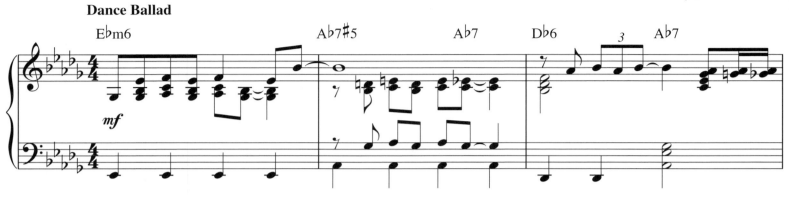

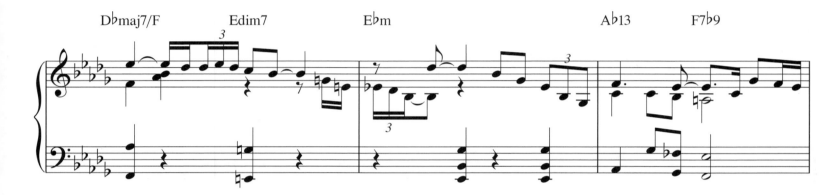

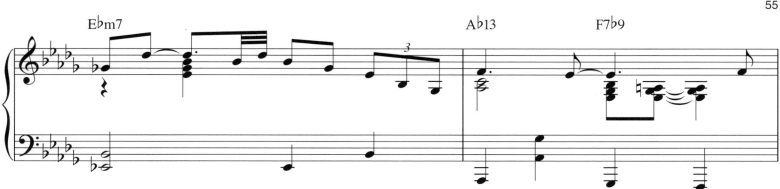

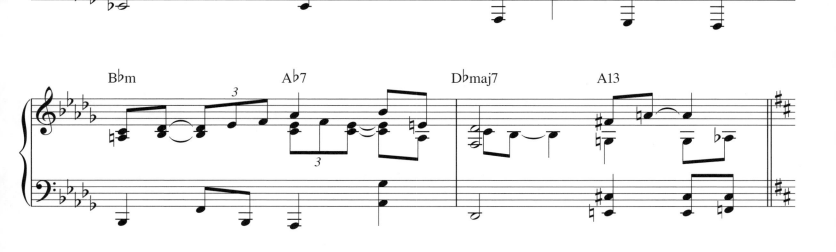

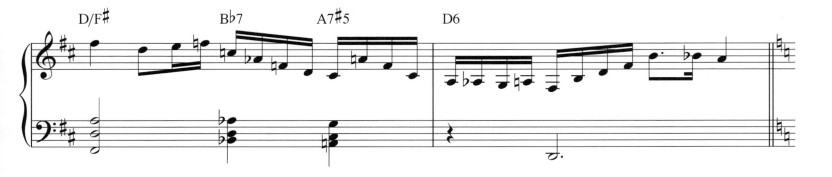

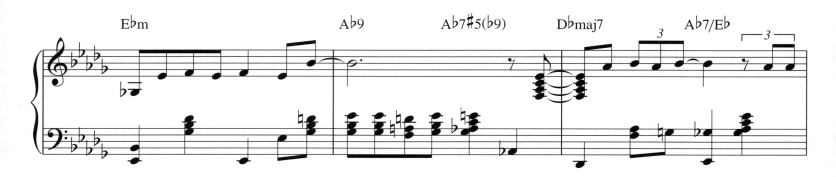

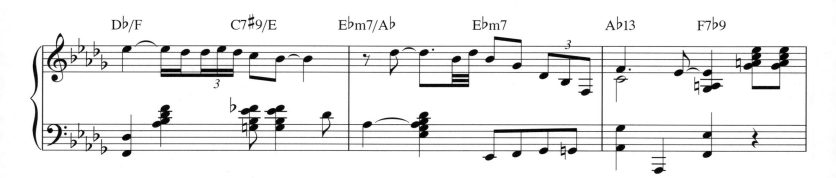

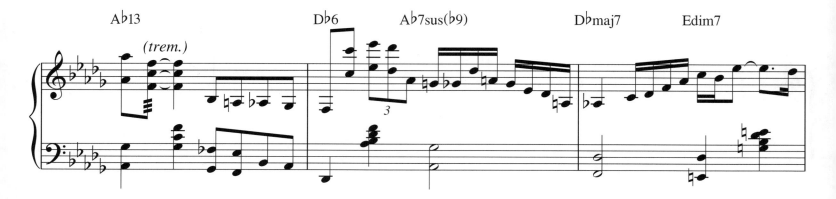

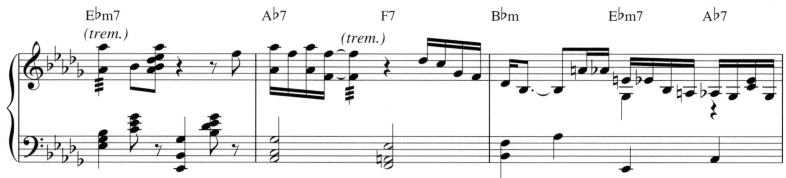

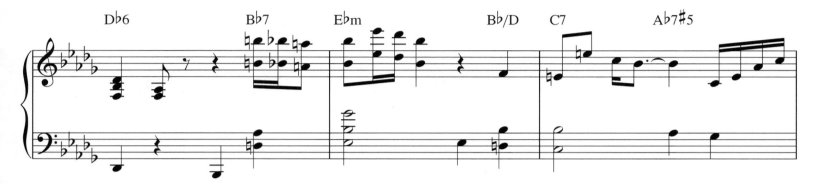

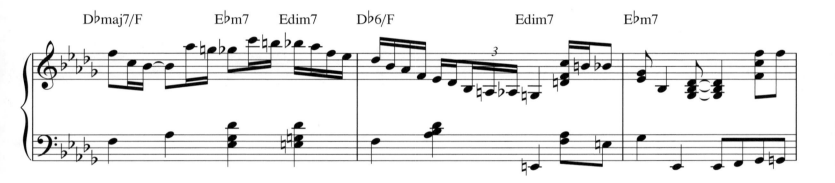

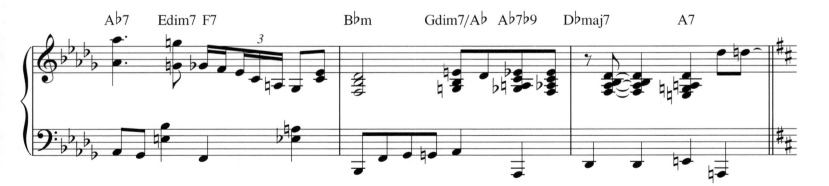

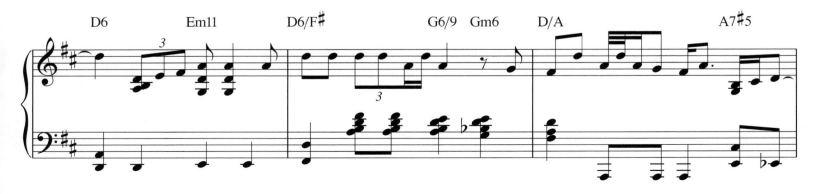

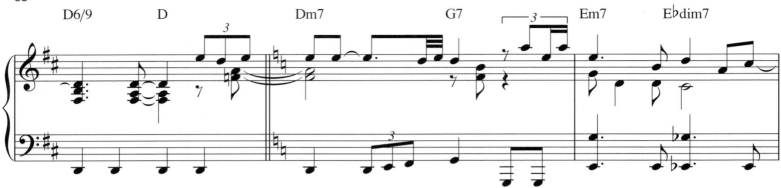

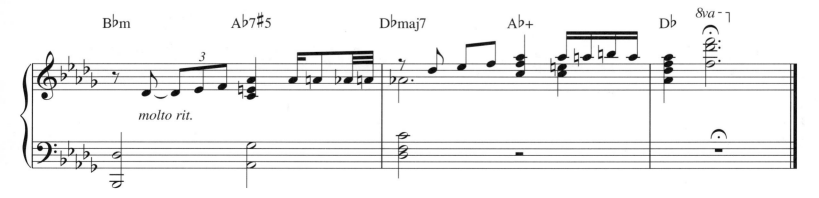

DARN THAT DREAM

Lyric by EDDIE DE LANGE
Music by JIMMY VAN HEUSEN

Moderate Dance tempo

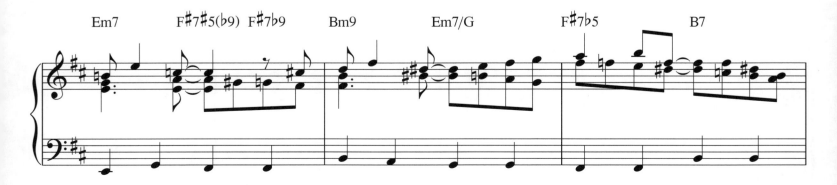

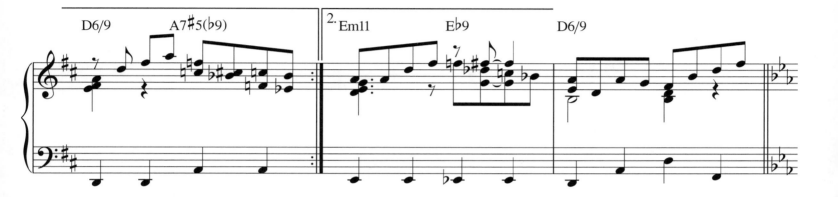

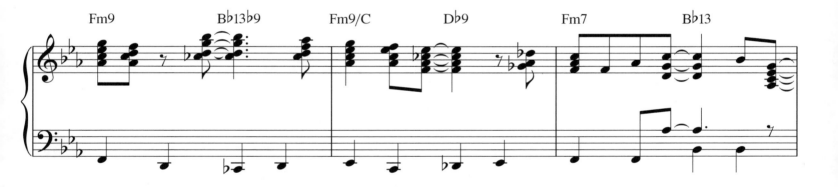

Darn that dream I dream each night. _
Darn your lips and darn your eyes. _

62

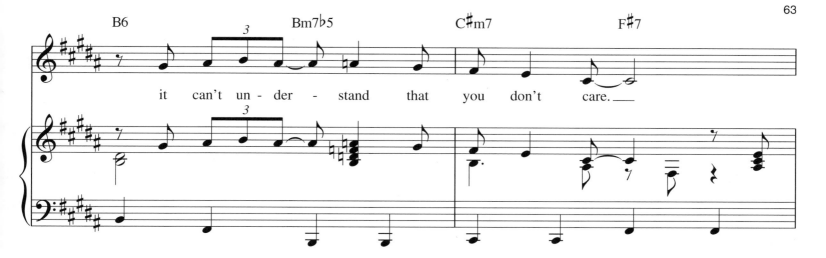

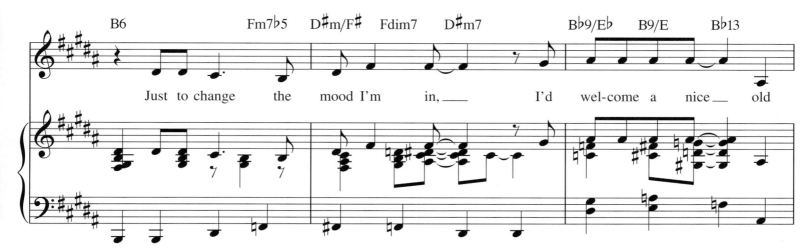

64

But it haunts me ____ and it won't come true, oh, ____ darn ___ that

dream. ____

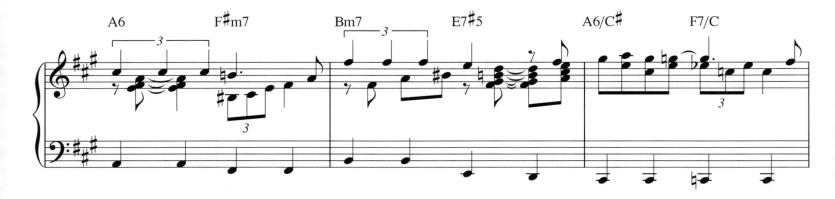

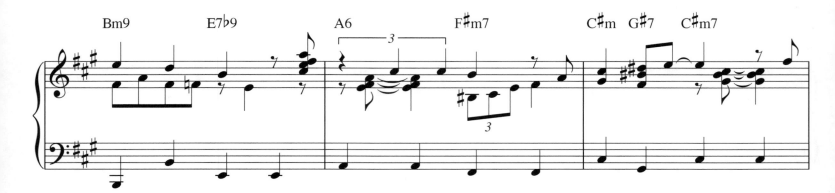

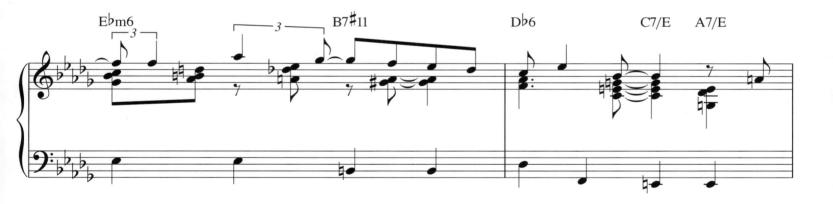

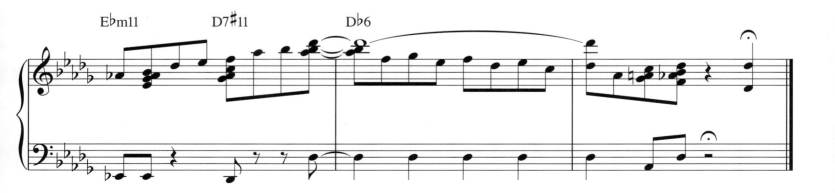

THE EARL

Words and Music by
MEL POWELL

Bright tempo

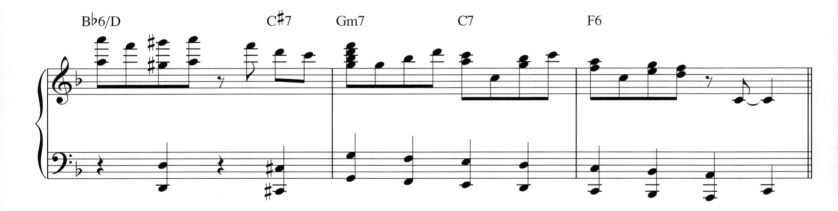

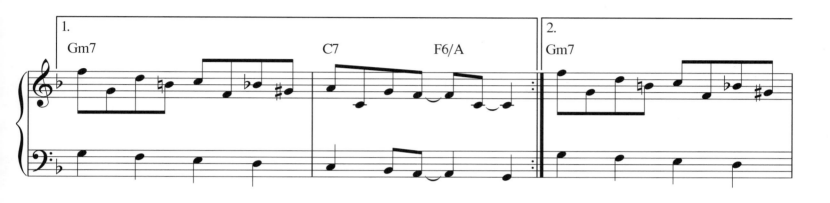

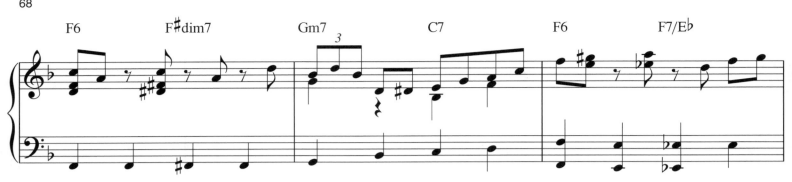

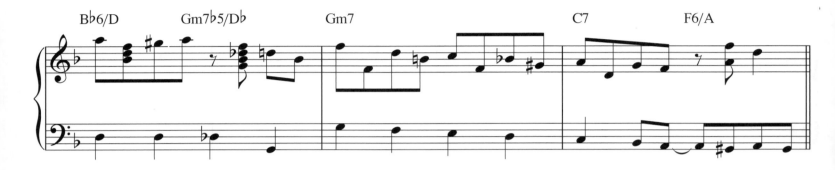

Ab7#11

G6/9

Saxophone solo-ad lib.

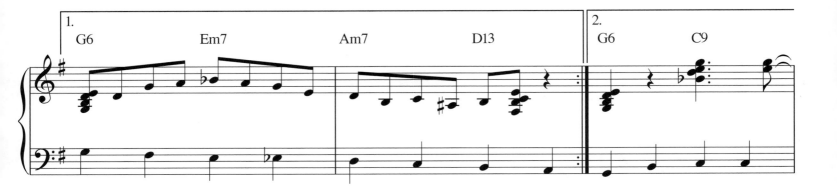

71

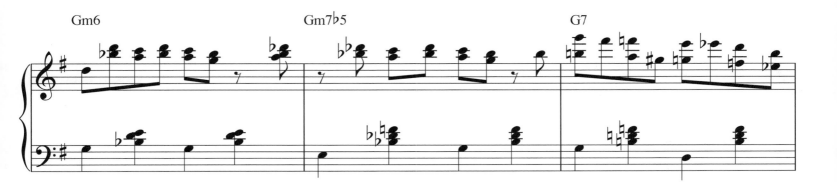

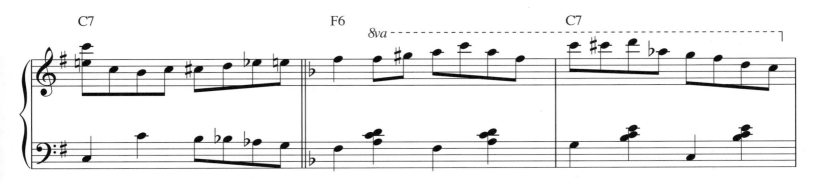

72

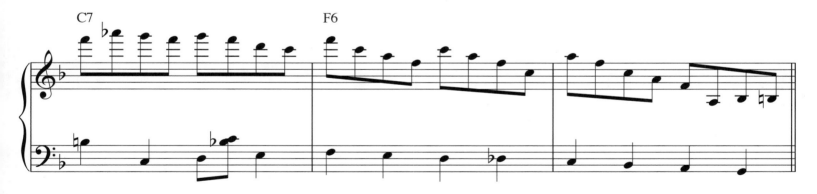

74

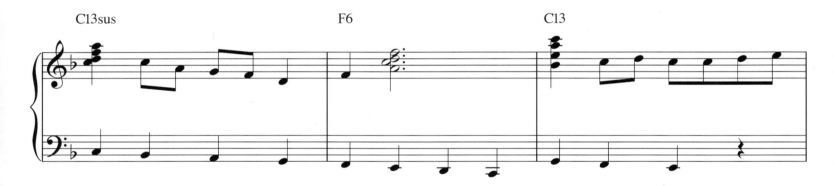

FLYING HOME

Music by BENNY GOODMAN
and LIONEL HAMPTON

Moderate Bounce

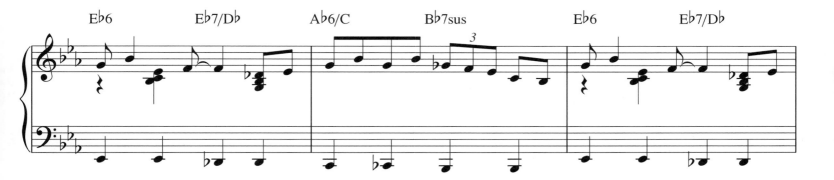

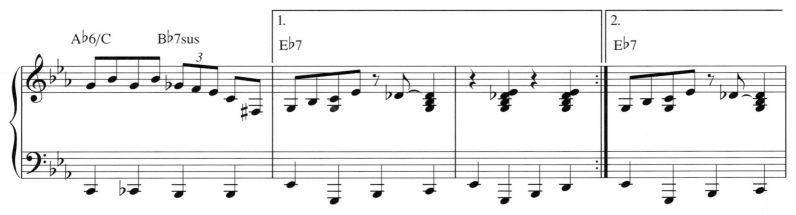

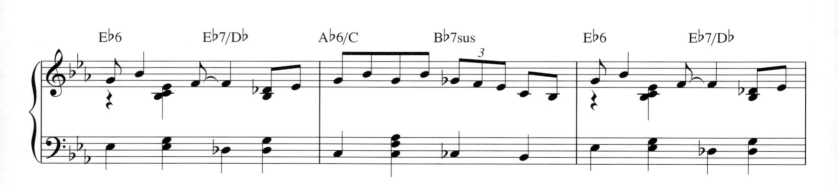

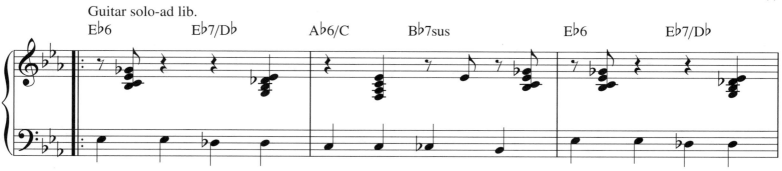

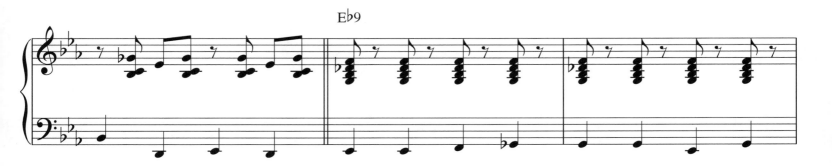

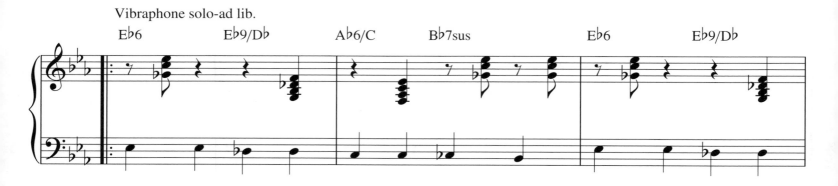

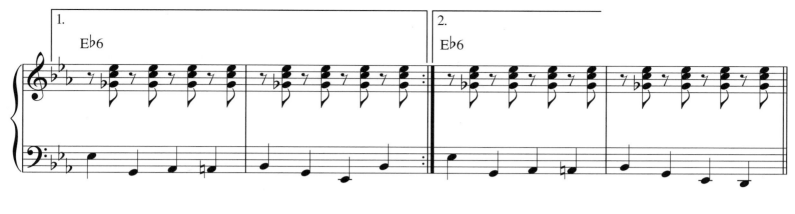

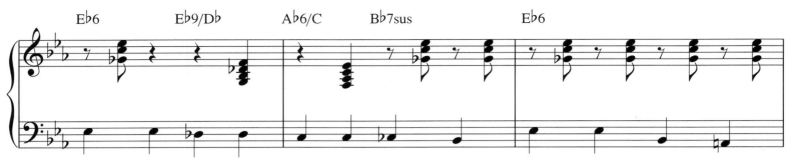

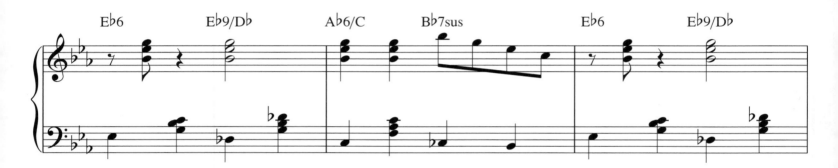

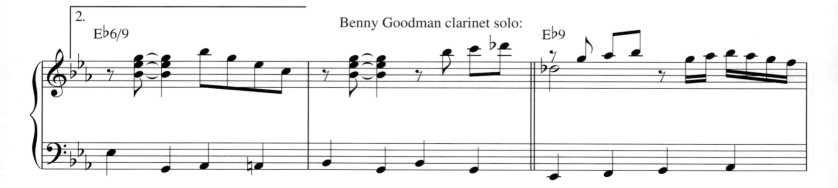

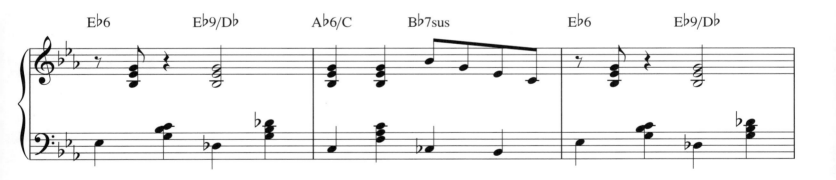

GOODBYE

Words and Music by
GORDON JENKINS

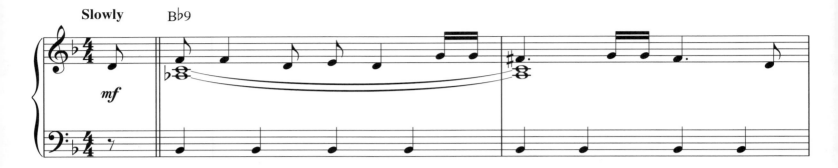

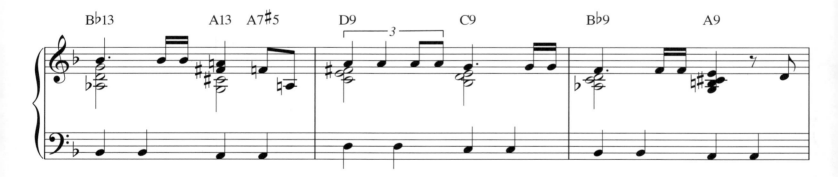

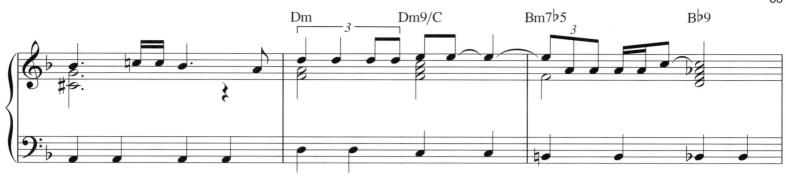

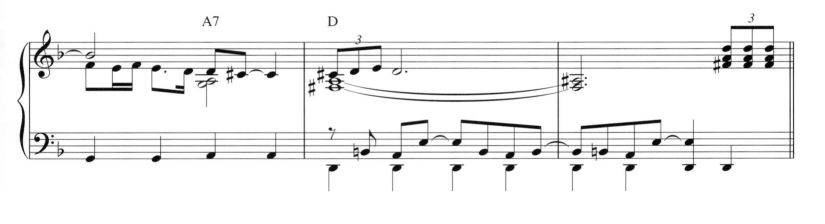

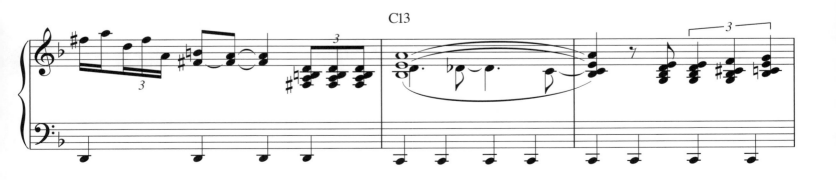

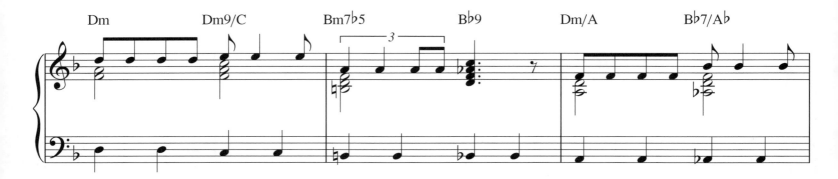

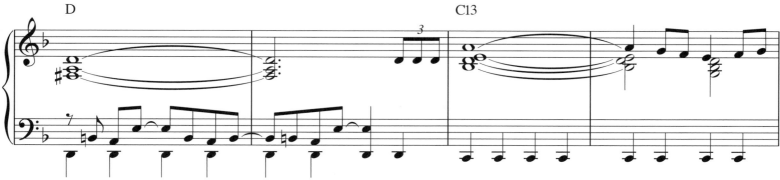

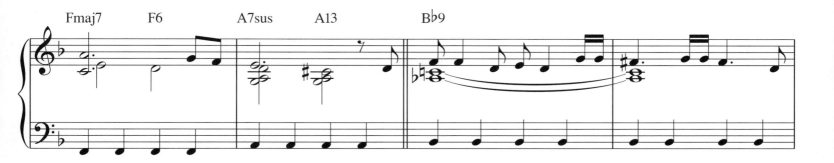

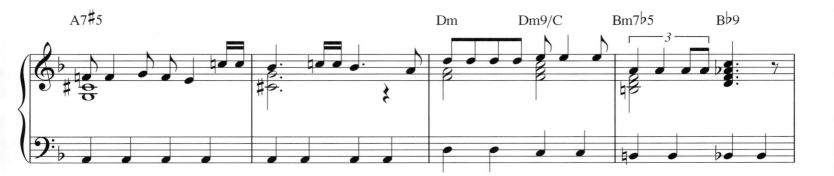

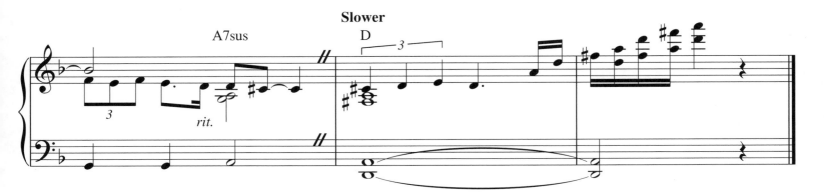

GOTTA BE THIS OR THAT

Words and Music by
SUNNY SKYLAR

Medium Dance tempo

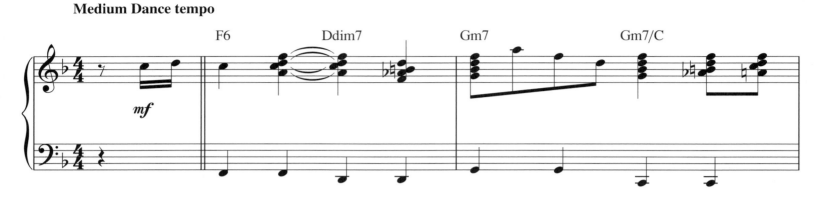

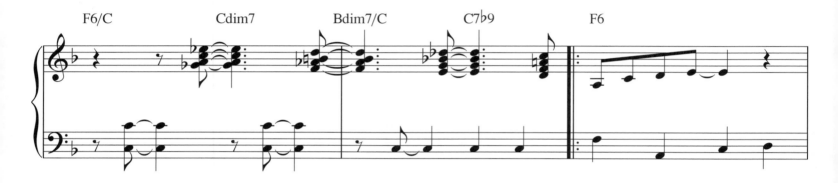

Jane Harvey:

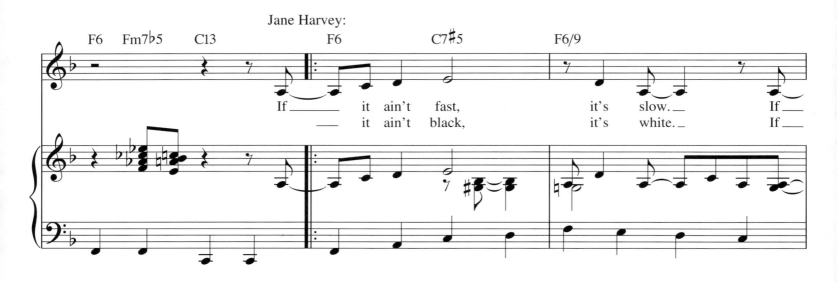

If _____ it ain't fast, it's slow. _____ If _____
_____ it ain't black, it's white. _ If

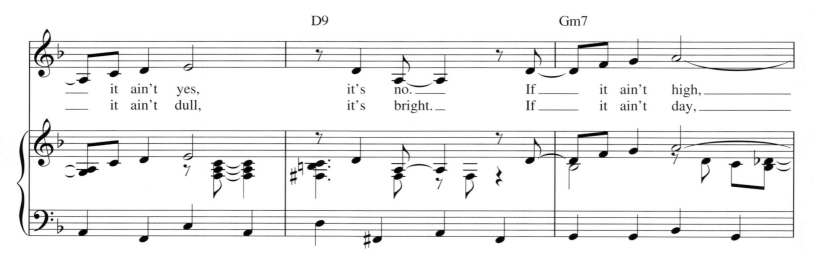

_____ it ain't yes, it's no. _____ If _____ it ain't high, _____
_____ it ain't dull, it's bright. _ If _____ it ain't day, _____

_____ it's low. _ Got - ta be this or _____ that. If _
_____ it's night. _ Got -

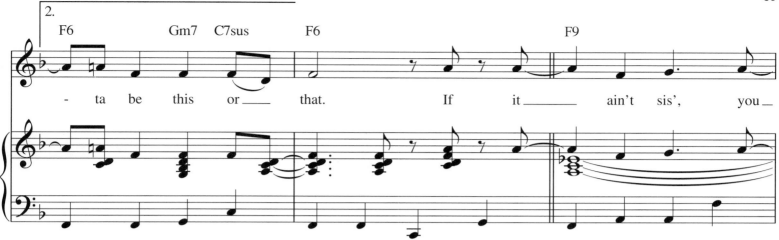

it ain't who, it's what. __ If __ you don't spend, __

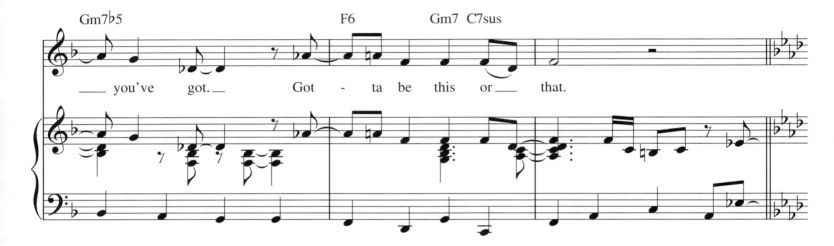

__ you've got. __ Got - ta be this or __ that.

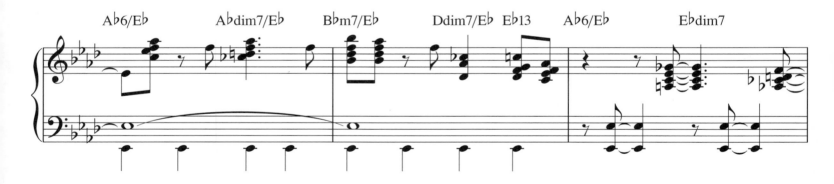

Benny Goodman:

If you ain't wrong, __ you're right. __
If you ain't dry, ___ it's wet. __

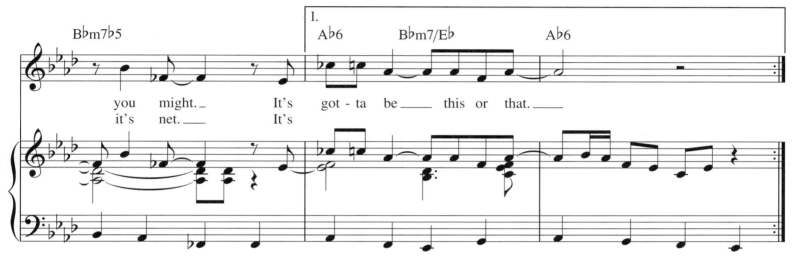

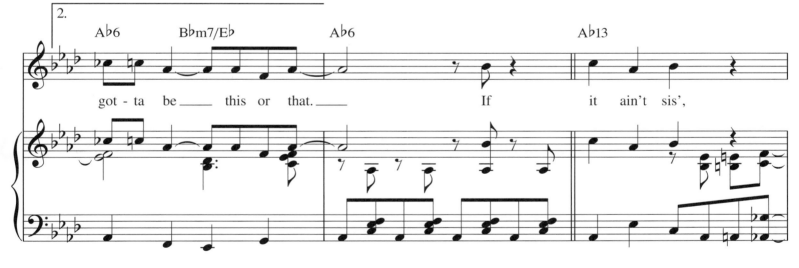

you see, _____ it's got to be _____ one way _____ or the

oth - er? ___ If it ain't full, it's blank. ___

If you don't spend, you bank. ___ If it ain't be, it's frank. ___

Got-ta be this ___ or that. _____

KING PORTER STOMP

By FERD "JELLY ROLL" MORTON

Bright Swing

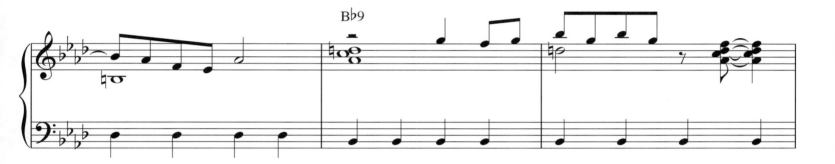

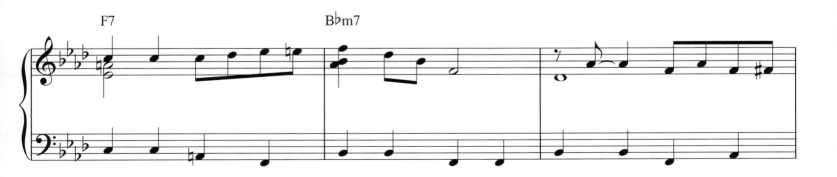

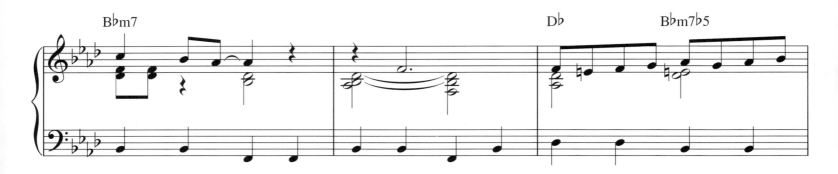

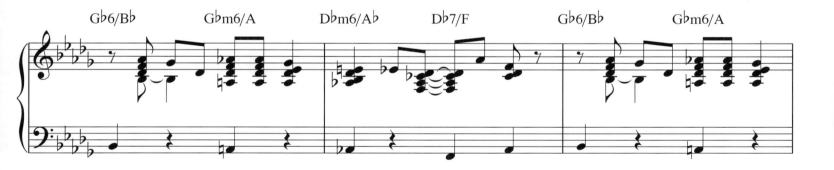

Benny Goodman clarinet solo:

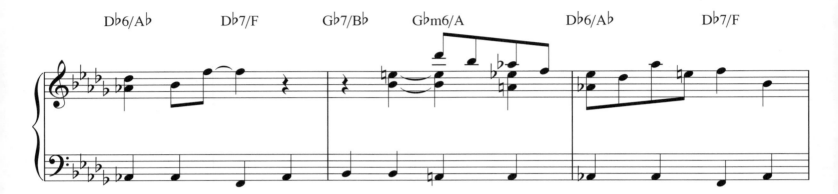

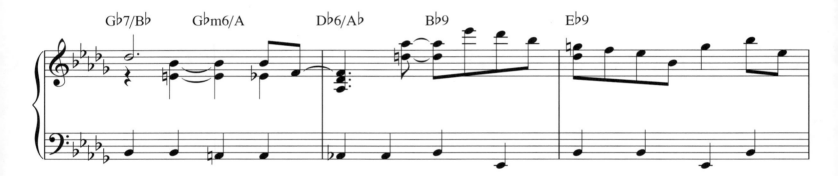

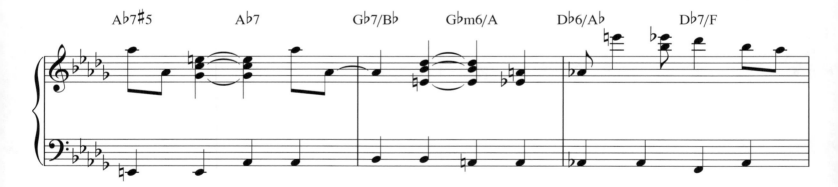

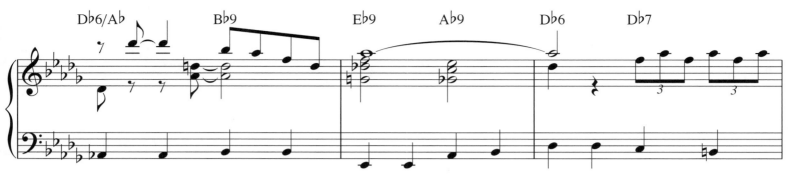

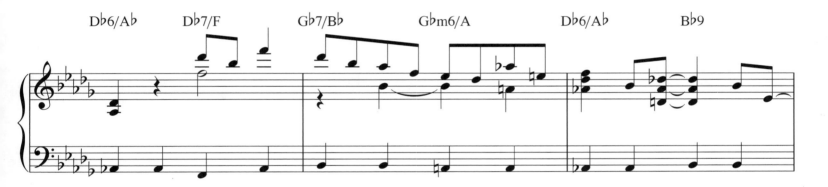

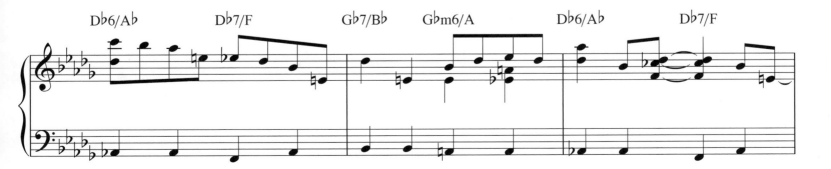

Trumpet solo-ad lib.

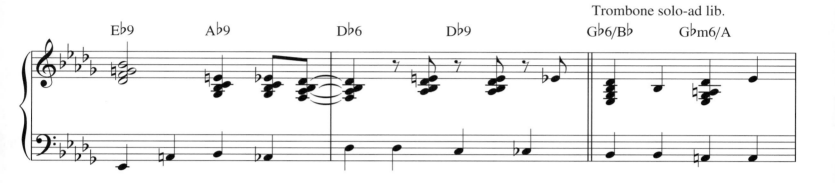

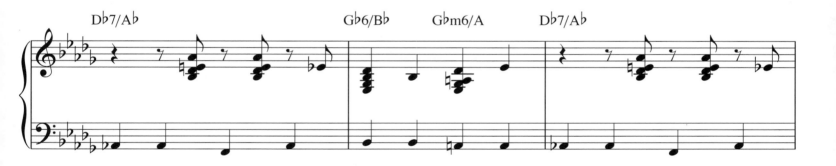

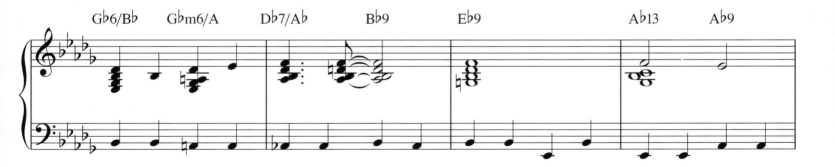

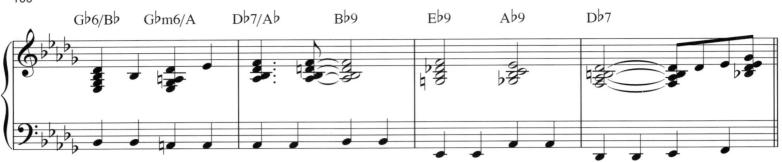

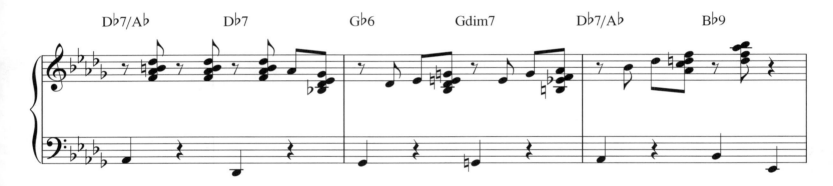

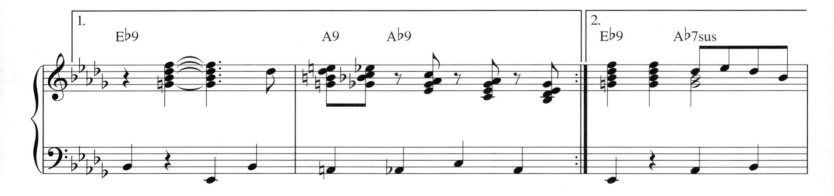

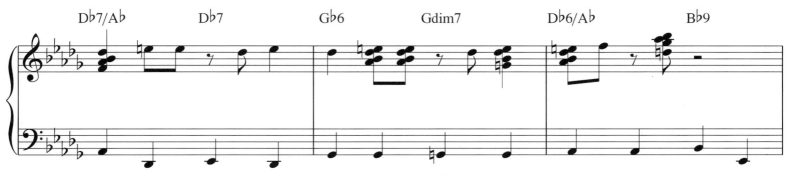

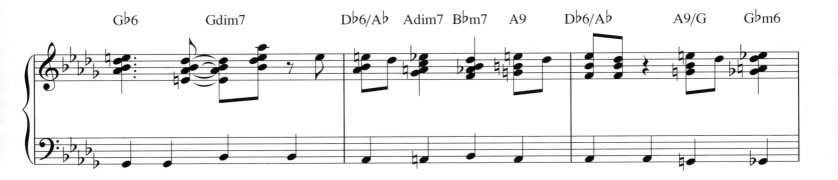

I'M HERE

Words and Music by
MEL POWELL

Medium Swing

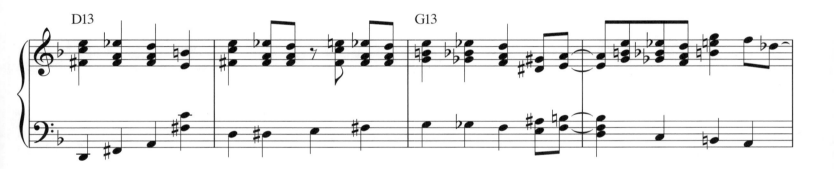

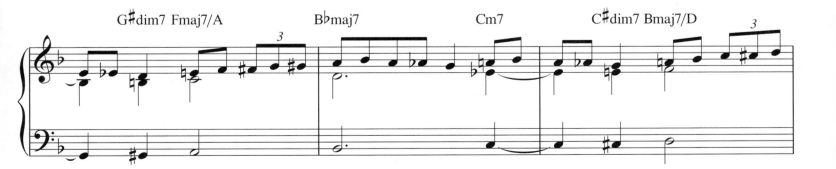

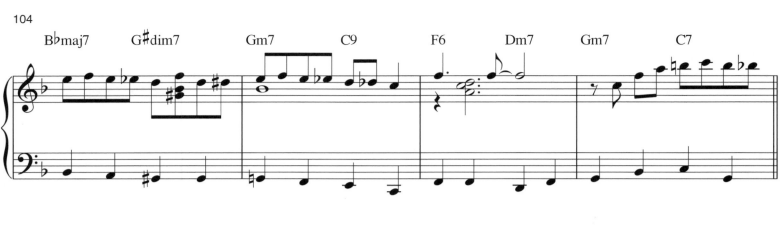

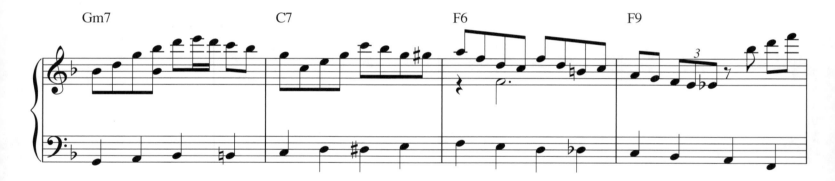

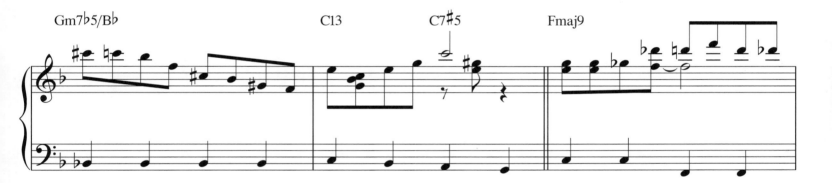

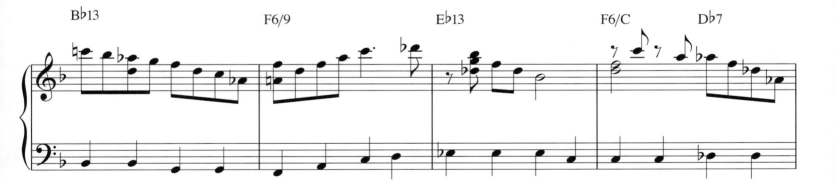

Trumpet solo-ad lib.

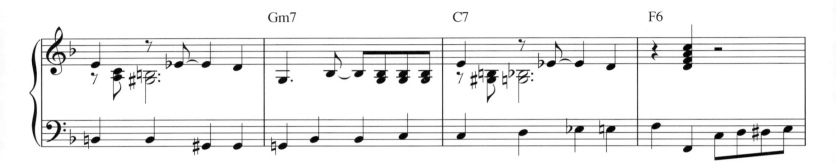

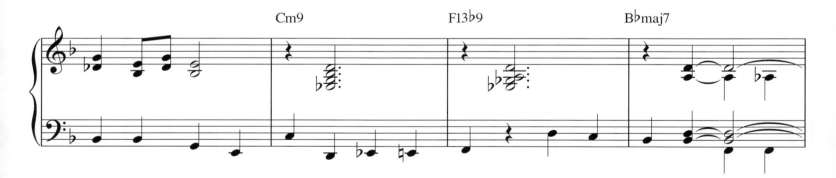

Trombone solo-ad lib.

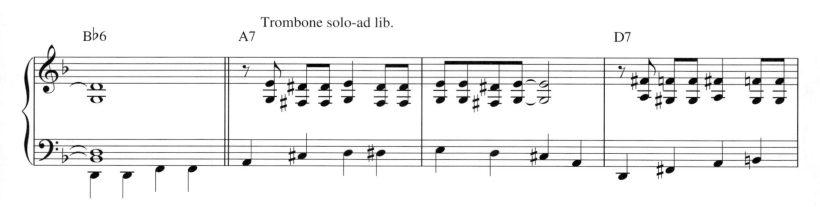

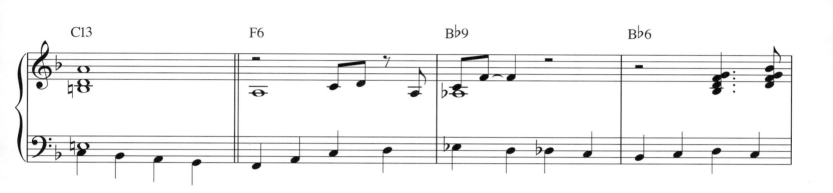

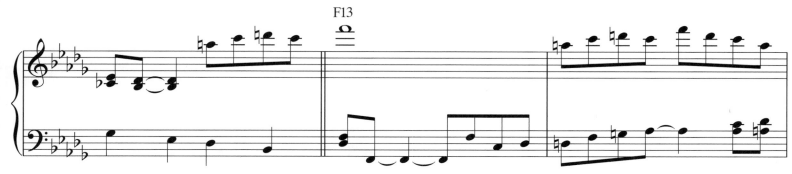

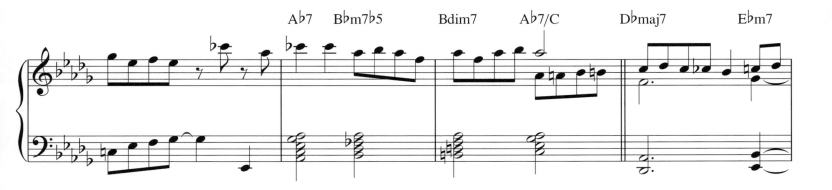

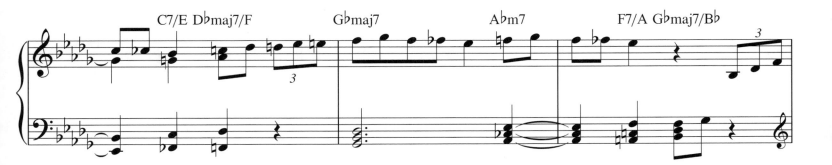

JERSEY BOUNCE

Words by ROBERT WRIGHT
Music by BOBBY PLATTER, TINY BRADSHAW,
ED JOHNSON and ROBERT WRIGHT

Medium Swing

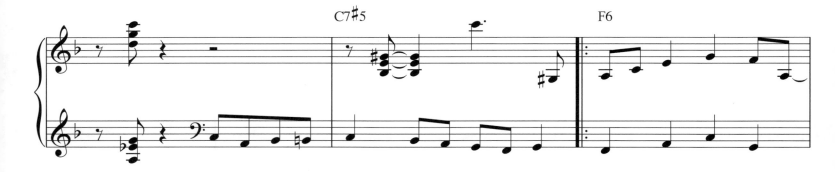

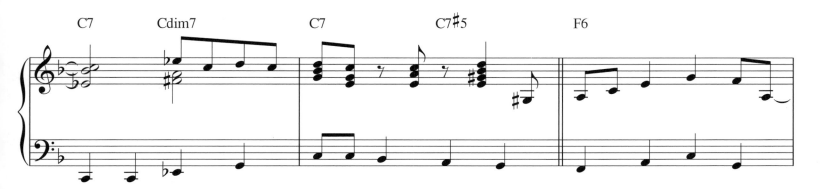

112

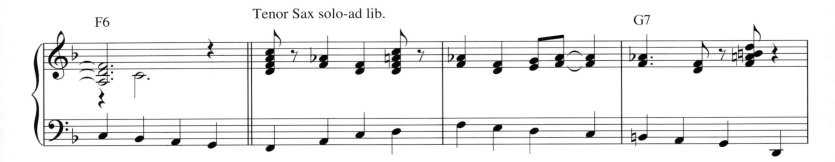

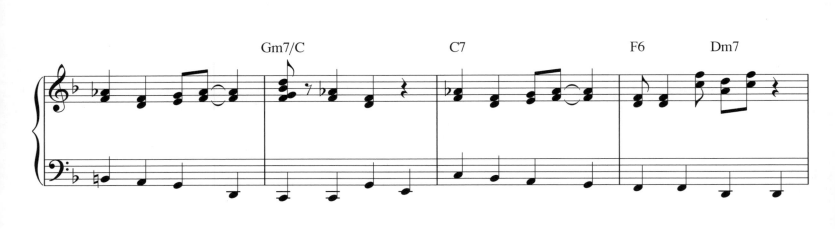

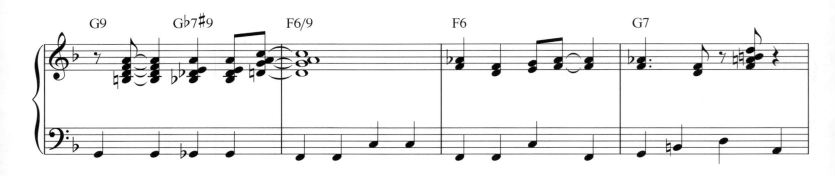

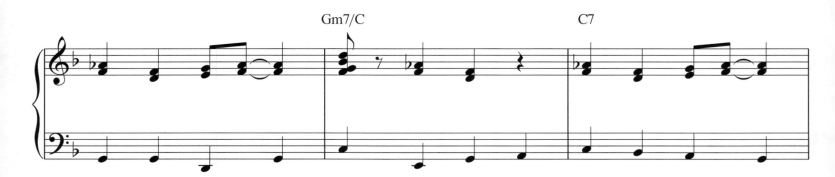

Benny Goodman clarinet solo:

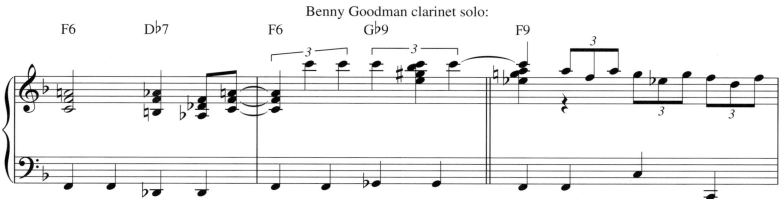

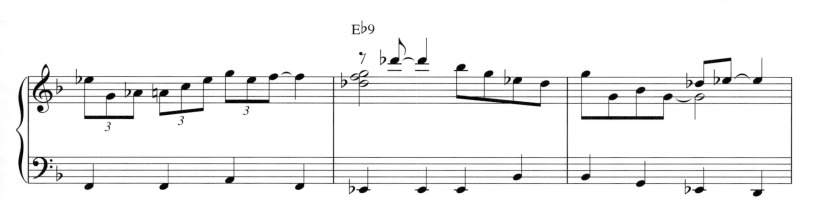

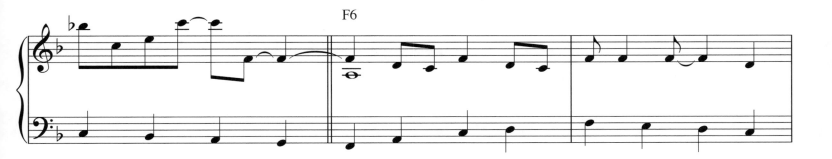

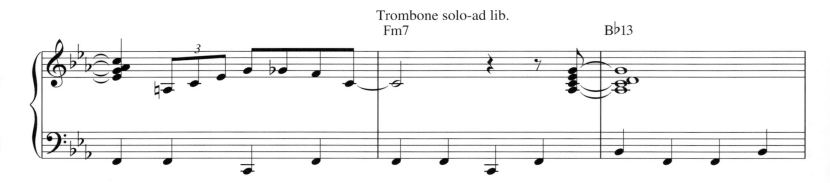

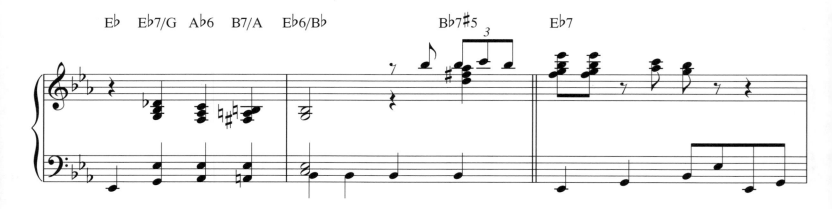

B13   B13♭9   B♭9

Trombone solo-ad lib.
E♭6

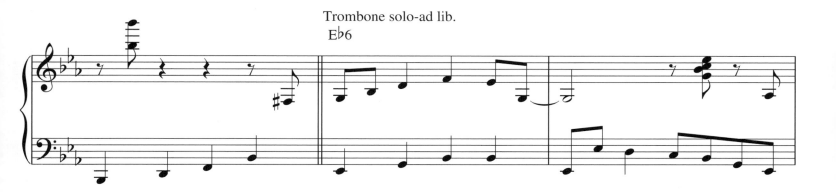

F9   Fm9/B♭

B♭13   E♭6   B9   E♭13

LET'S DANCE

Words by FANNY BALDRIDGE
Music by GREGORY STONE and JOSEPH BONINE

Bright Dance tempo

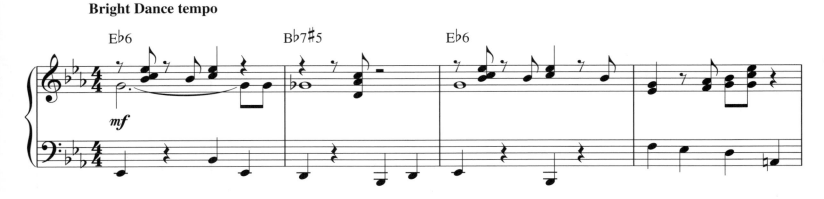

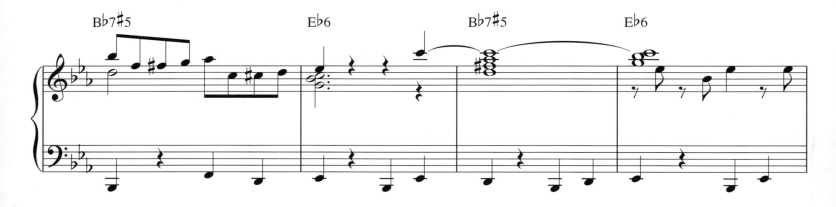

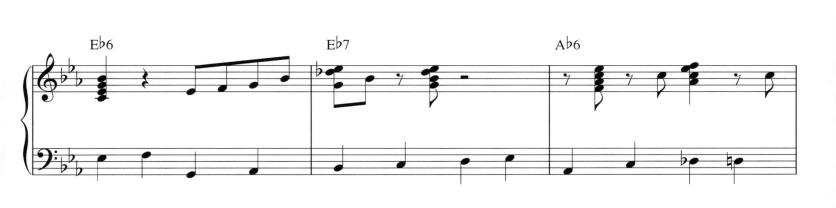

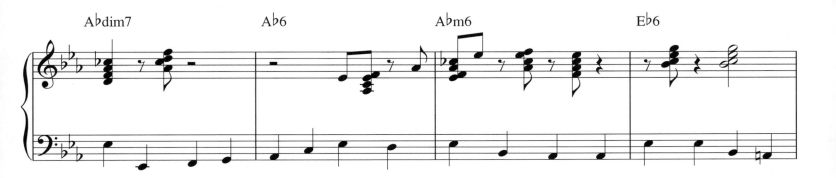

Benny Goodman clarinet solo:

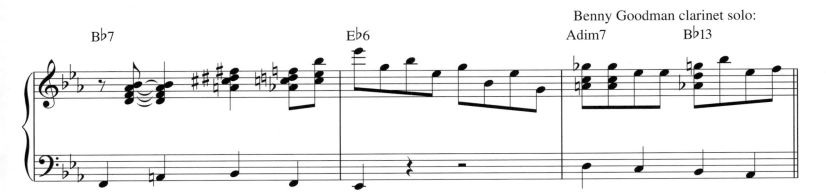

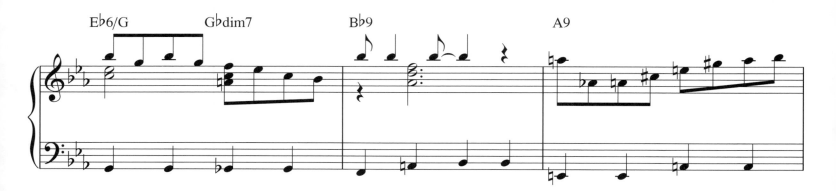

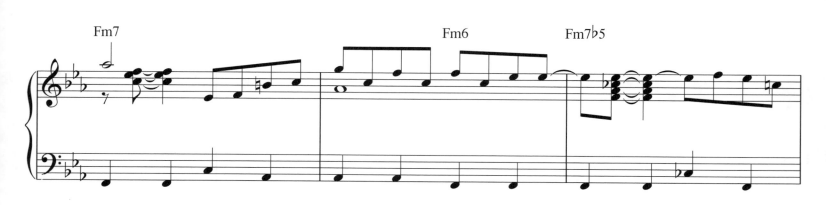

119

Saxophone solo:

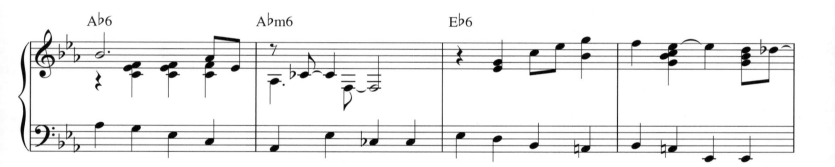

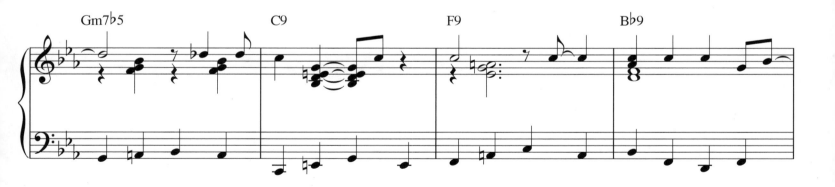

122

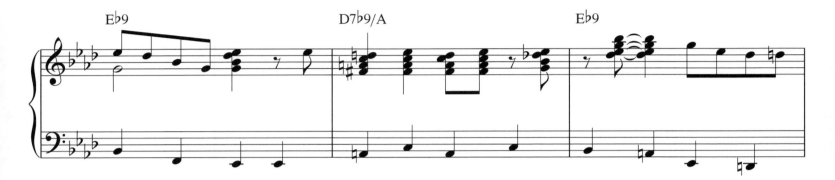

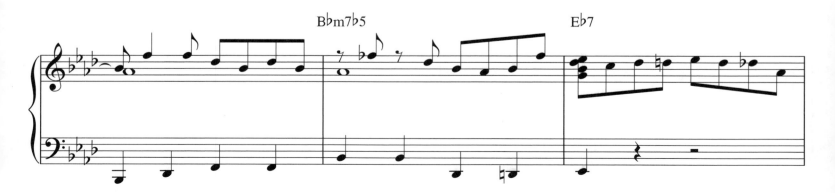

123

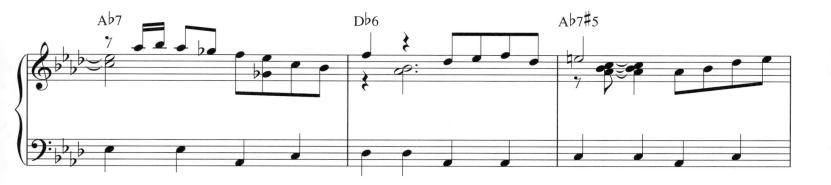

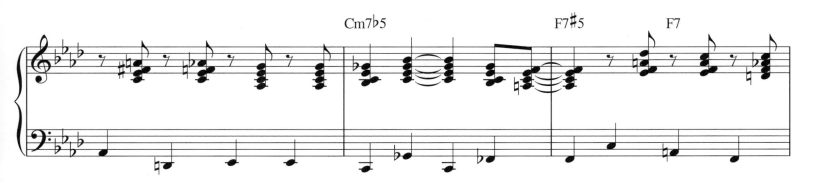

MISSION TO MOSCOW

By MEL POWELL

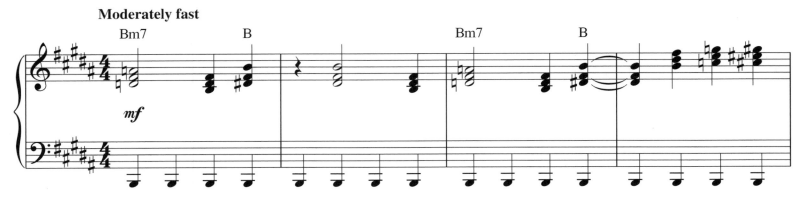

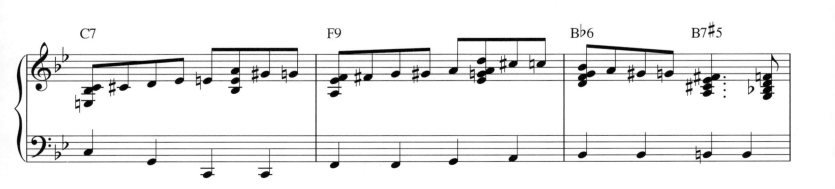

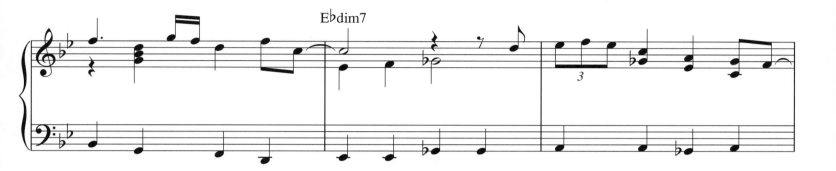

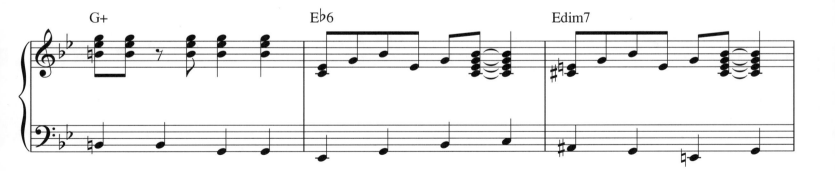

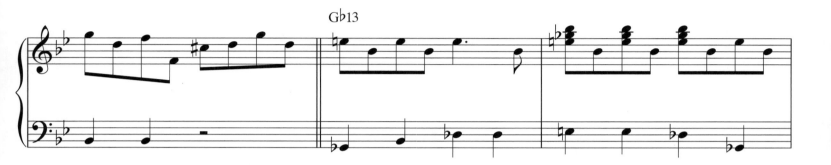

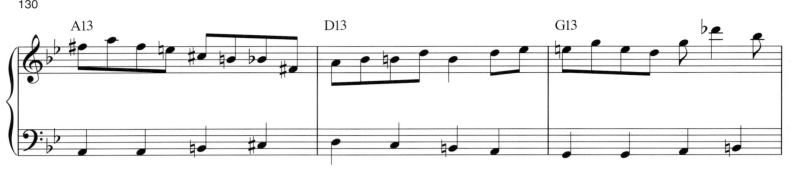

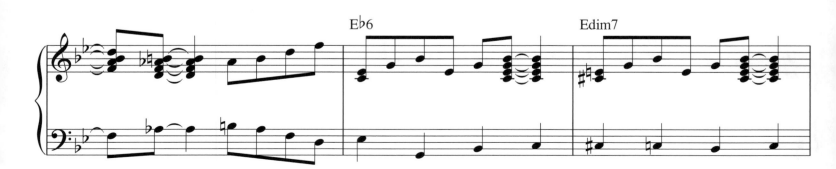

Benny Goodman clarinet solo:

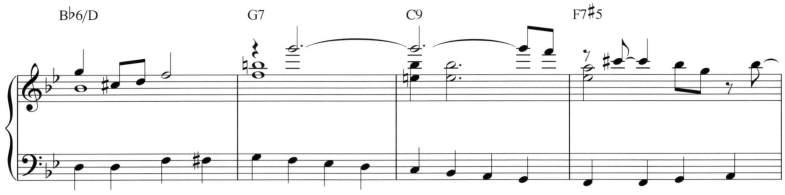

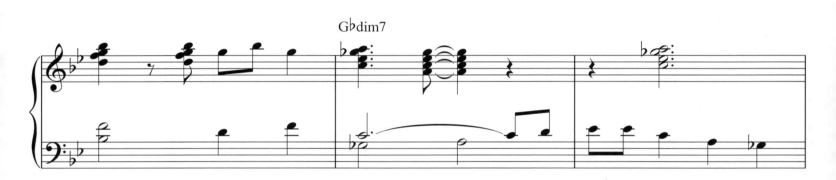

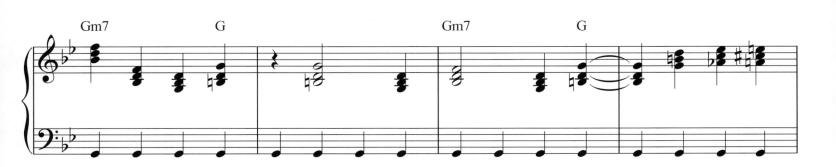

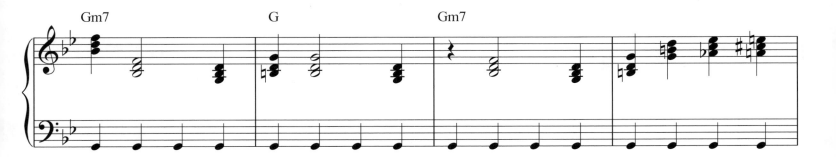

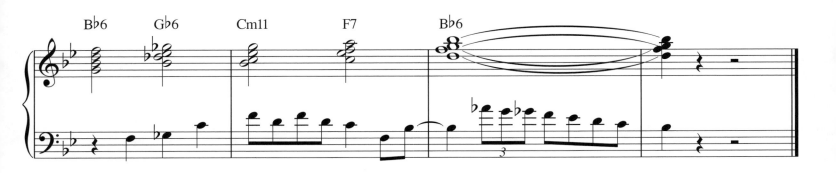

MOONGLOW

Words and Music by WILL HUDSON,
EDDIE DE LANGE and IRVING MILLS

Moderately slow

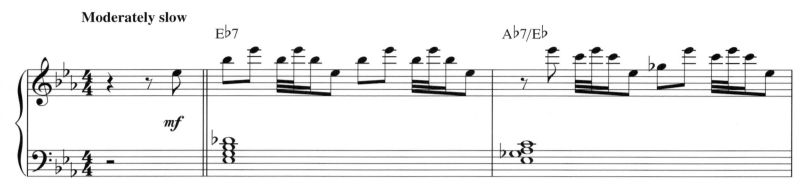

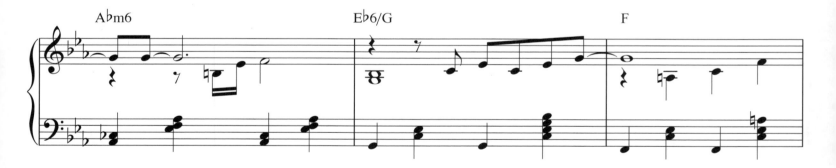

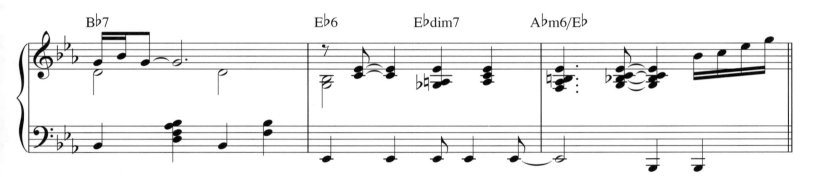

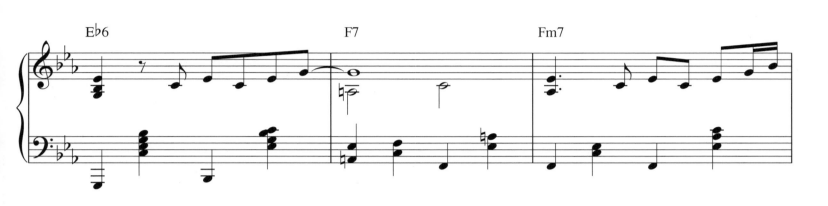

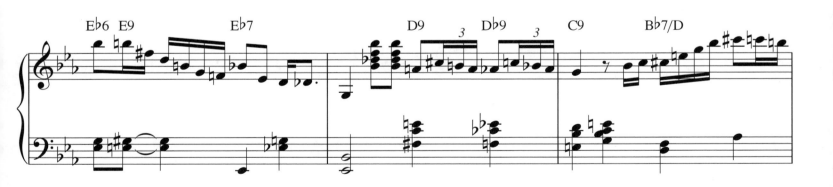

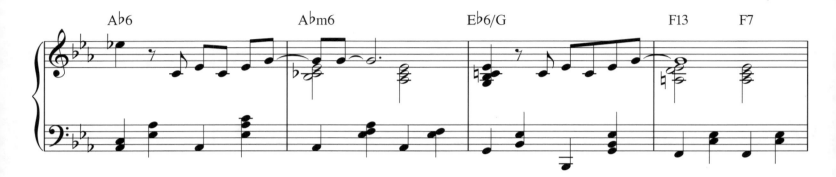

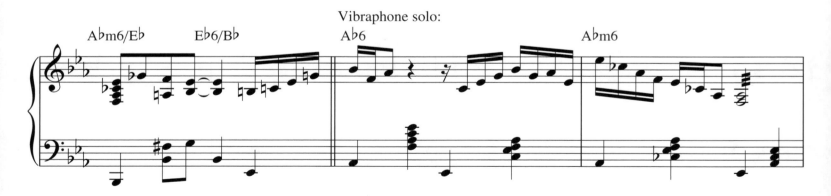

Vibraphone solo:

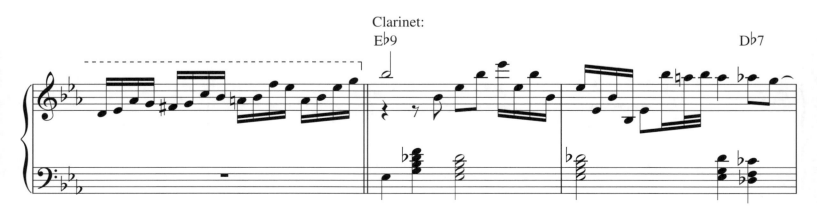

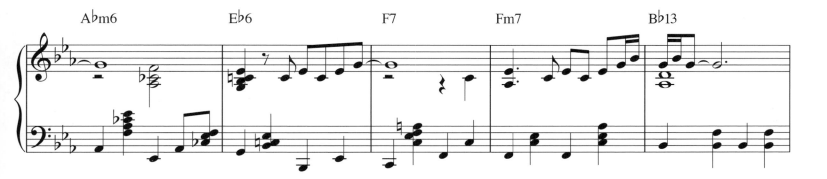

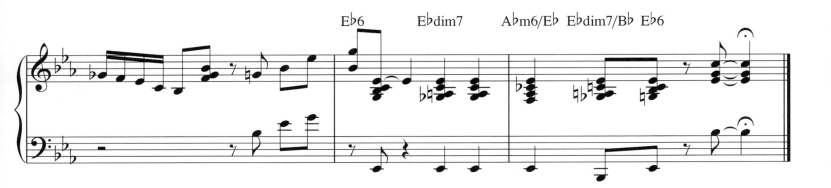

MORE THAN YOU KNOW

Words by WILLIAM ROSE and EDWARD ELISCU
Music by VINCENT YOUMANS

Moderate Ballad

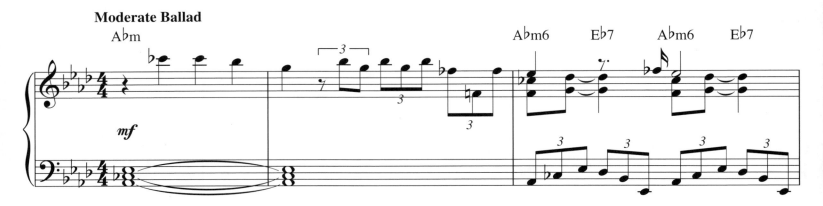

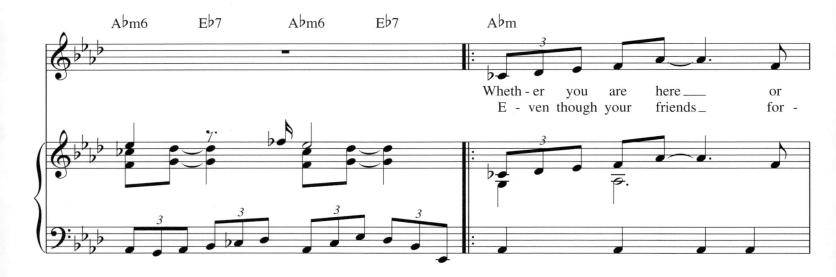

Wheth-er you are here ___ or
E - ven though your friends ___ for-

yon - der, wheth-er you are false ___ or true,
sake you, e - ven though you don't ___ suc - ceed,

noth - ing ___ I can do a - bout it. _____ Lov - ing may be

all you can give, but, Hon - ey, I can't ___ live with - out it. ___

Oh, how I'd cry, oh, how I'd sigh, if you got

tired and ___ said good - bye. More than I'd show, more than you'd

ev - er know.

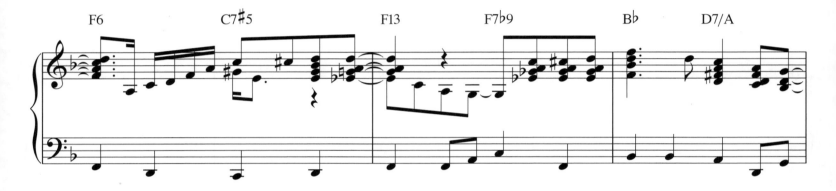

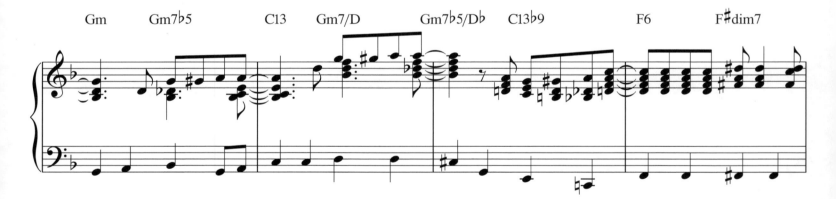

Benny Goodman clarinet solo:

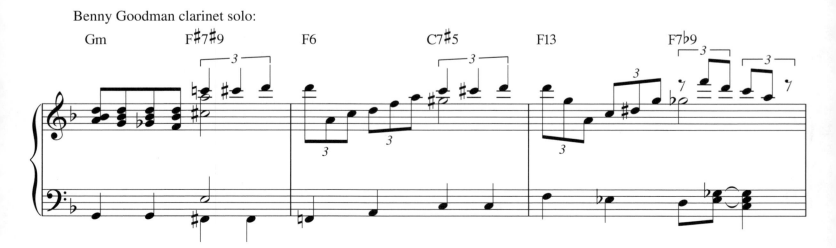

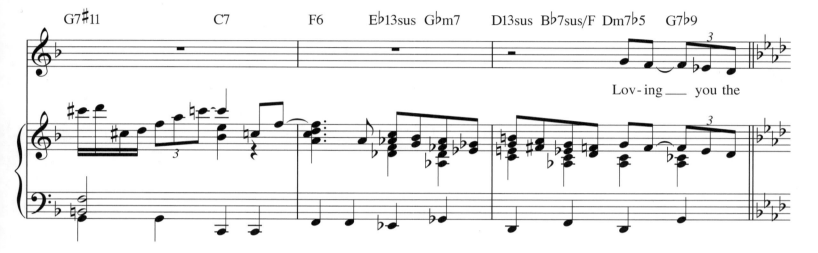

Lov-ing___ you the

way___ that I do, there's noth-ing___ I can do a - bout it.___

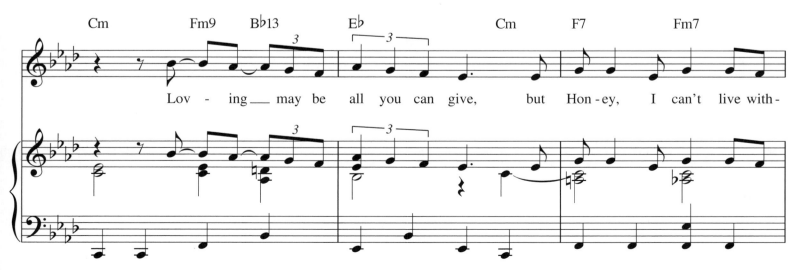

Lov - ing___ may be all you can give, but Hon - ey, I can't live with-

out it. — Oh, — how I'd cry, — oh, how I'd

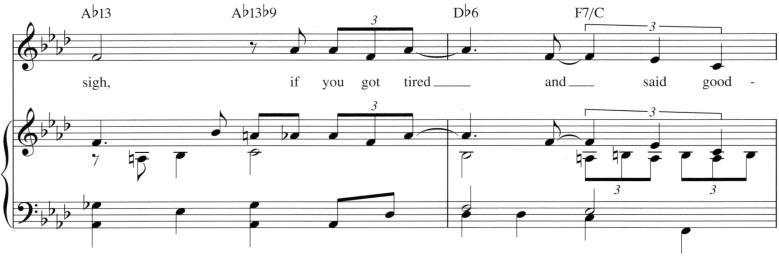

sigh, if you got tired — and — said good -

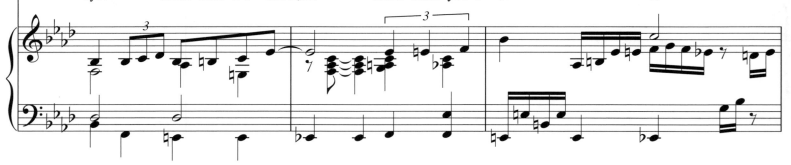

bye. More than I'd show, — more than you'd ev - er

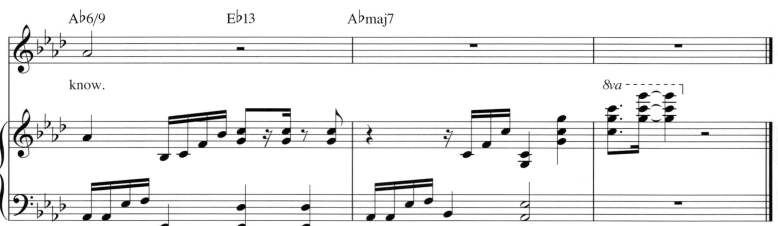

know.

STOMPIN' AT THE SAVOY

By BENNY GOODMAN,
EDGAR SAMPSON and CHICK WEBB

Moderate Dance tempo

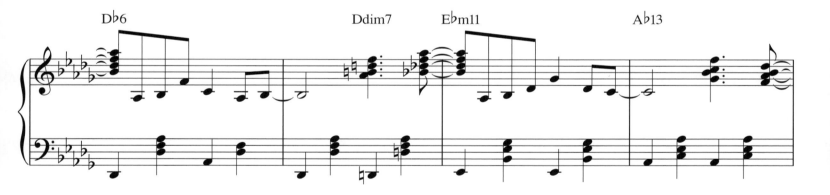

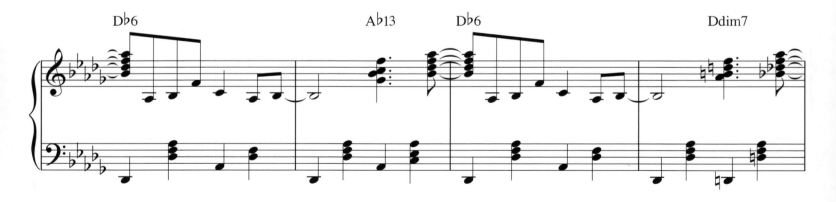

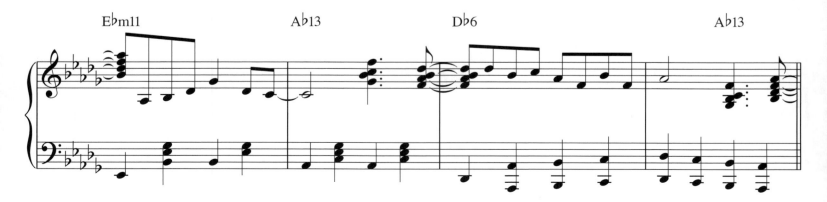

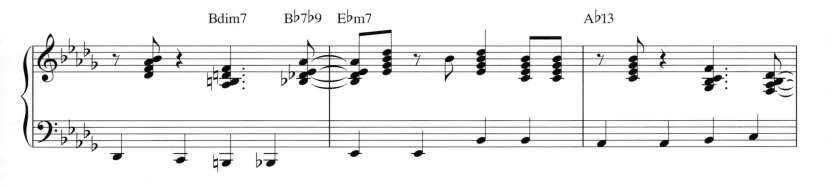

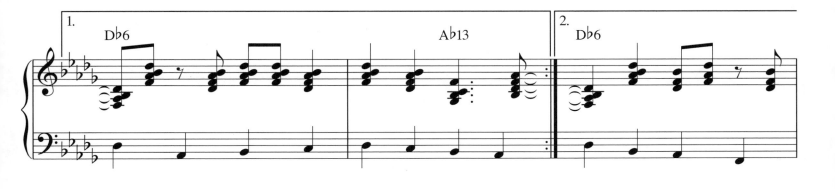

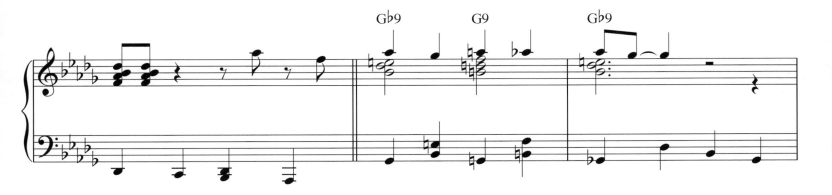

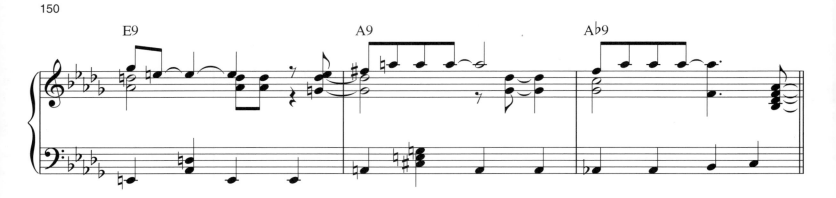

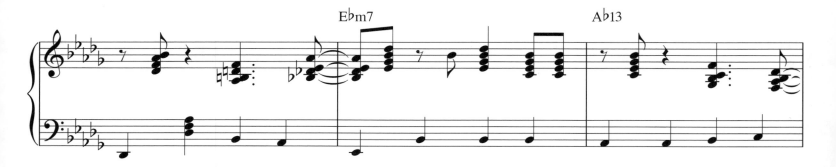

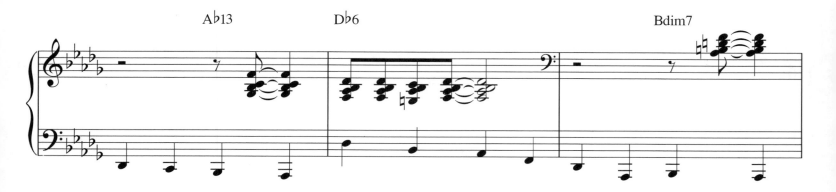

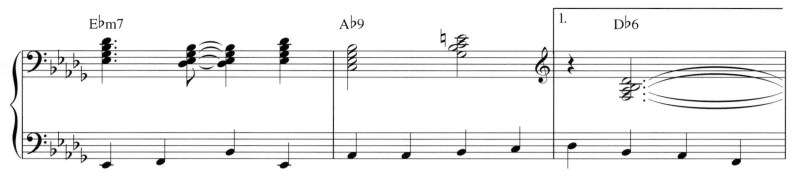

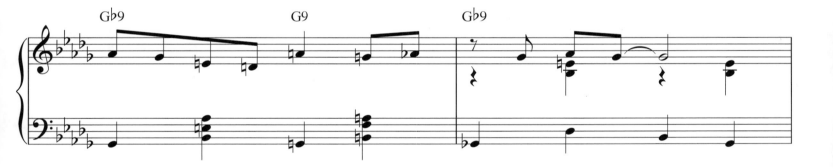

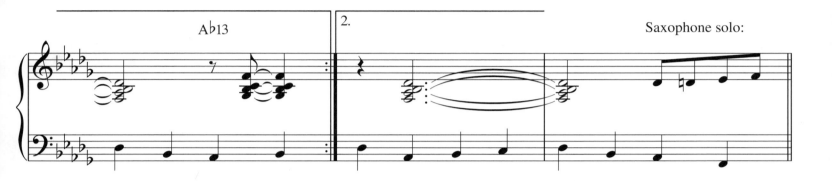

152

Trombone solo ad lib.

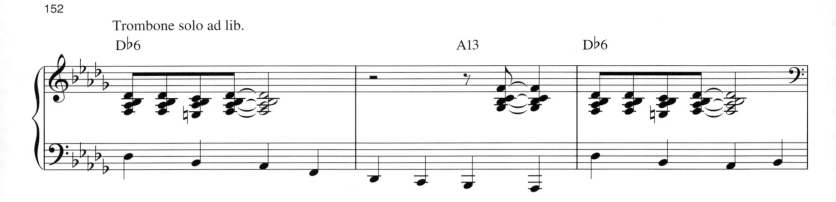

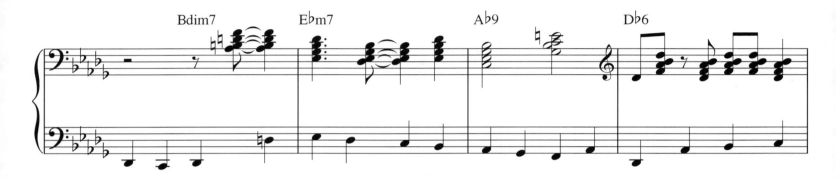

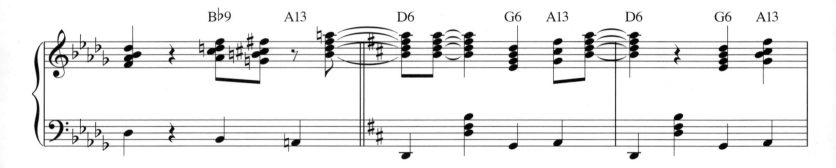

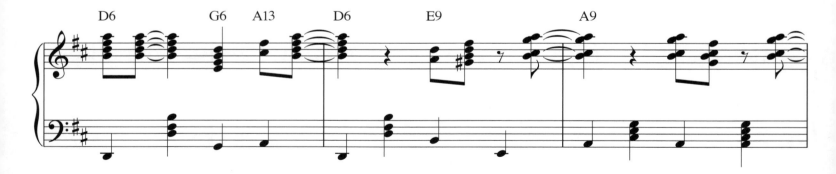

153

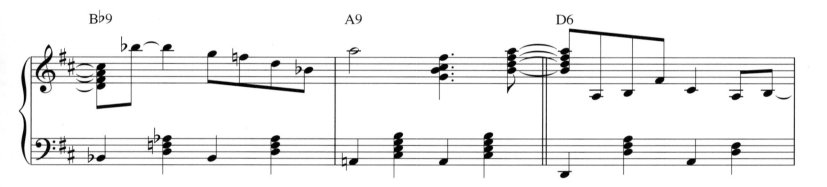

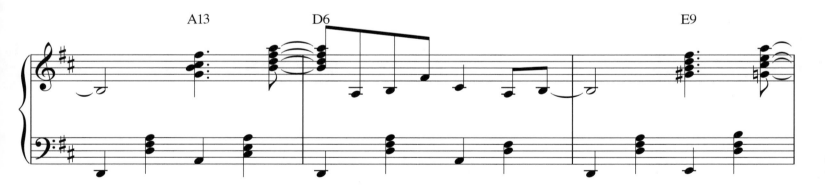

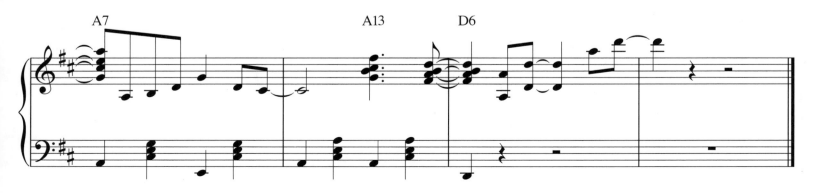

SEVEN COME ELEVEN

By BENNY GOODMAN
and CHARLIE CHRISTIAN

Bright Swing

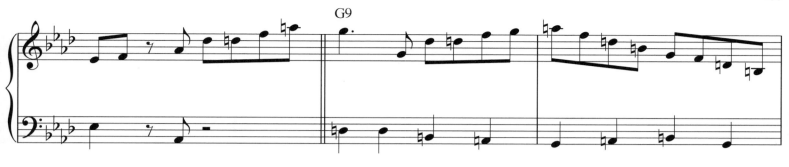

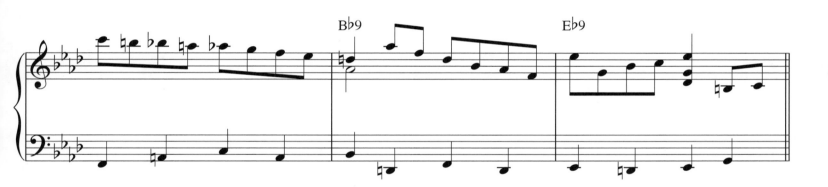

Guitar solo-ad lib.

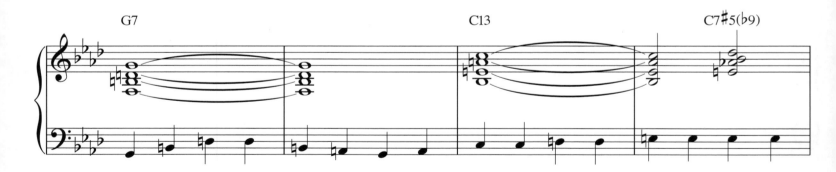

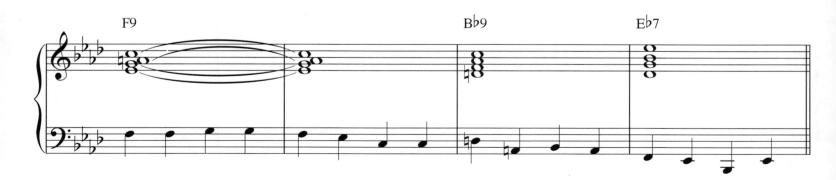

Vibraphone solo-ad lib.

Benny Goodman clarinet solo:

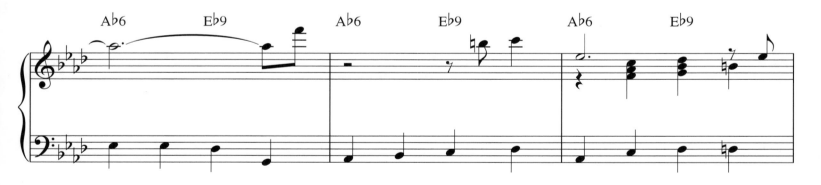

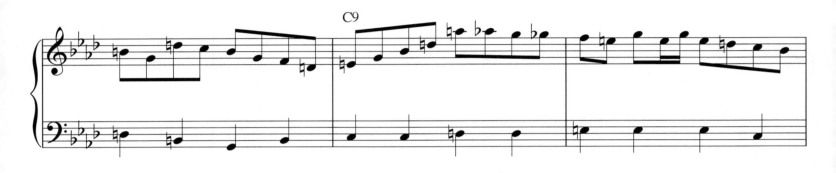

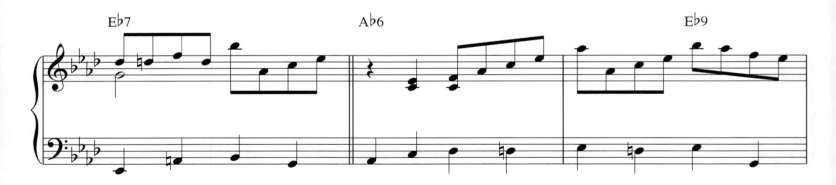

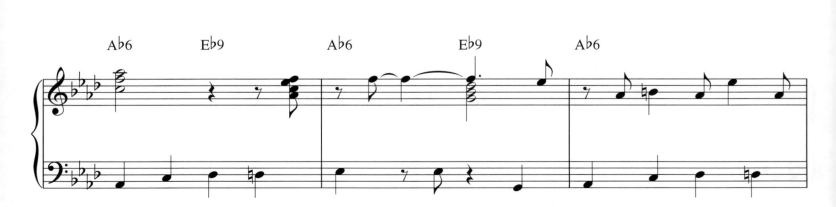

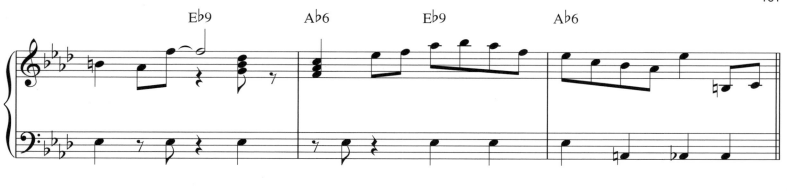

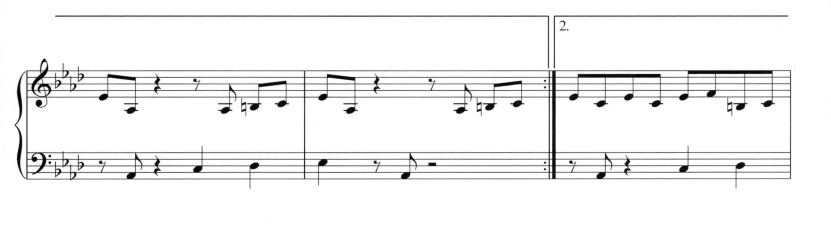

SING, SING, SING

Words and Music by
LOUIS PRIMA

Jungle Drum Swing

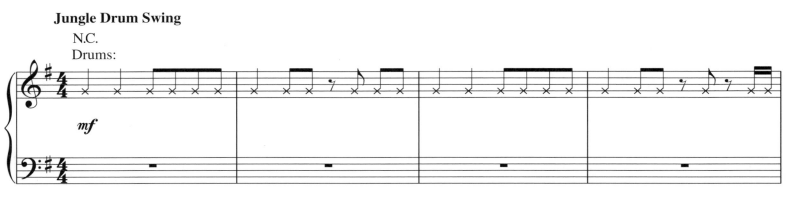

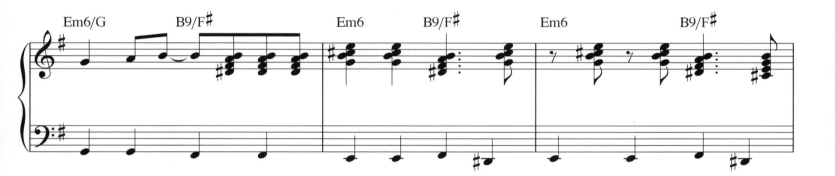

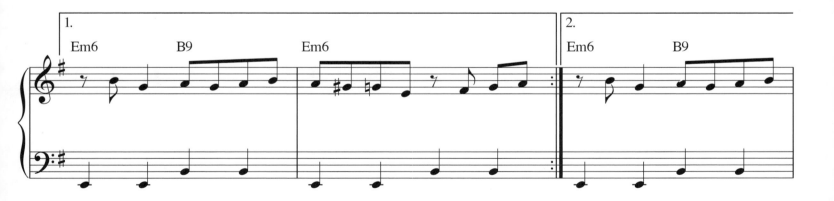

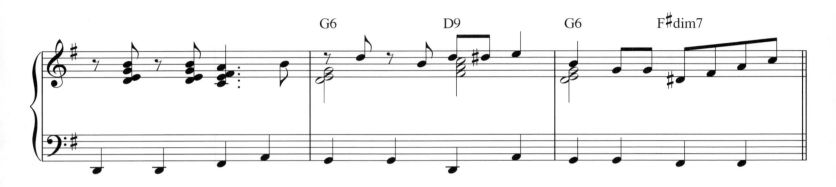

Benny Goodman clarinet solo:

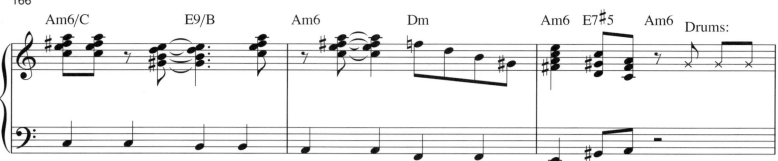

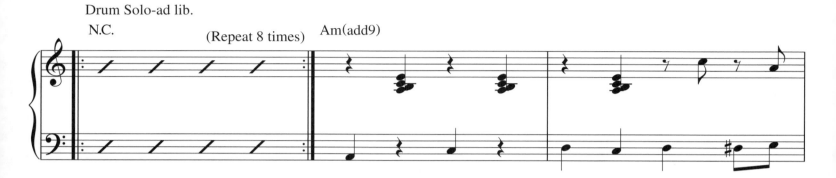

Drums:

1.-7.
Drum Solo-ad lib.
N.C.

8.

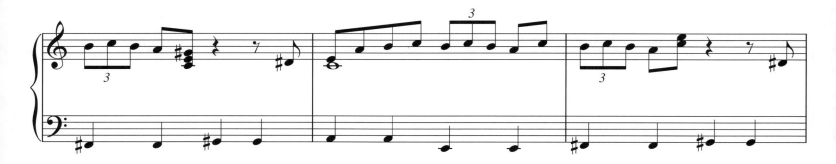

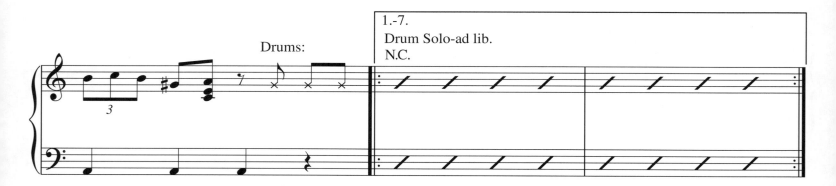

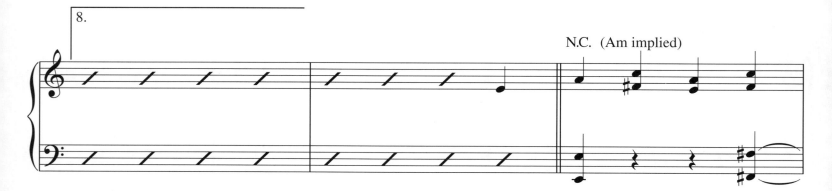

170

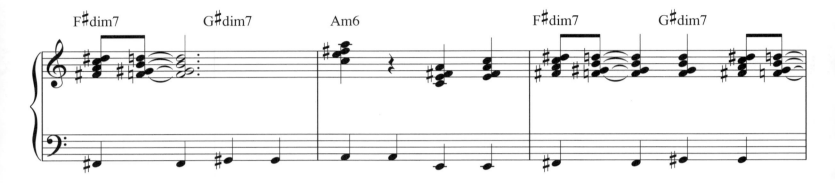

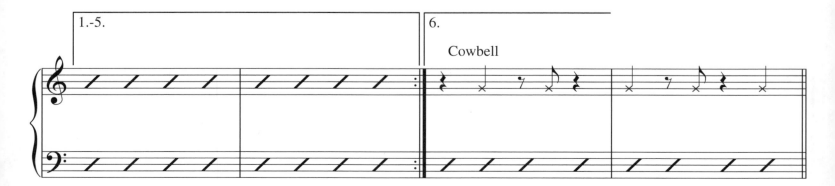

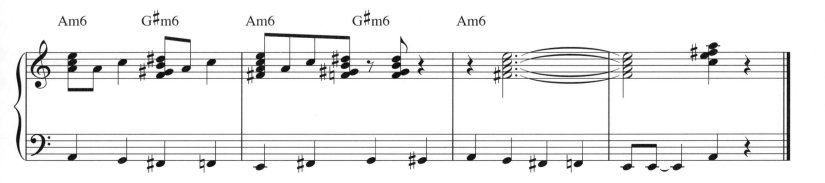

A SMOOTH ONE

By BENNY GOODMAN

Medium Dance tempo

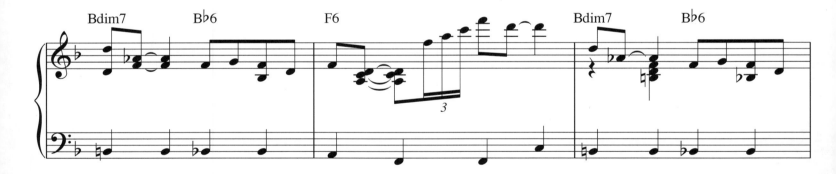

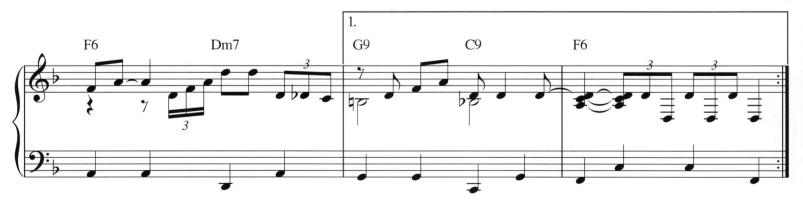

173

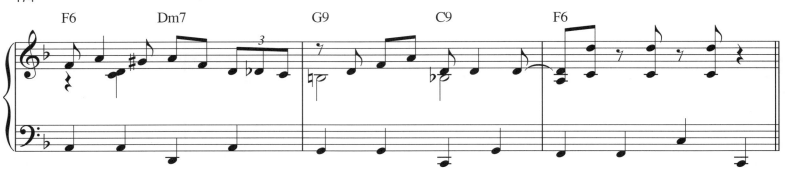

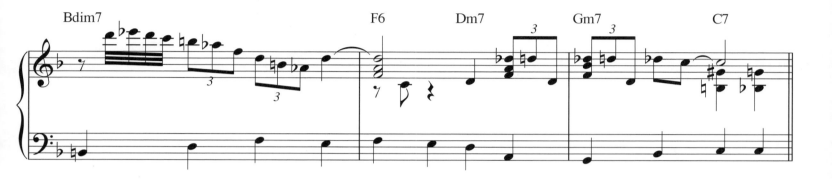

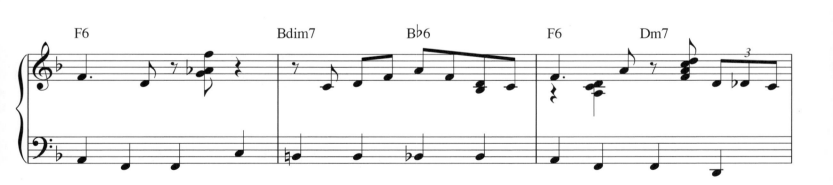

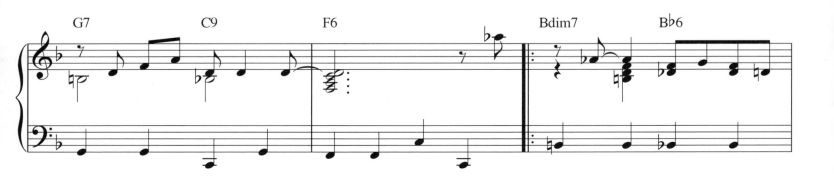

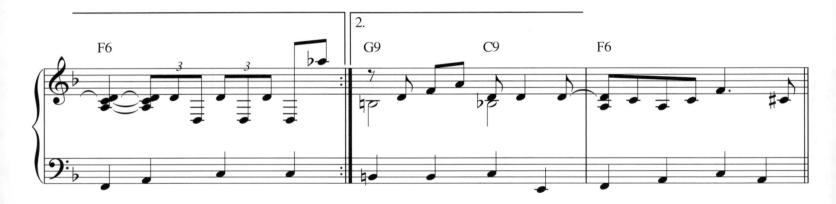

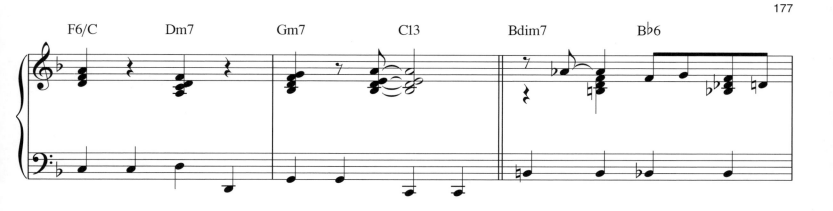

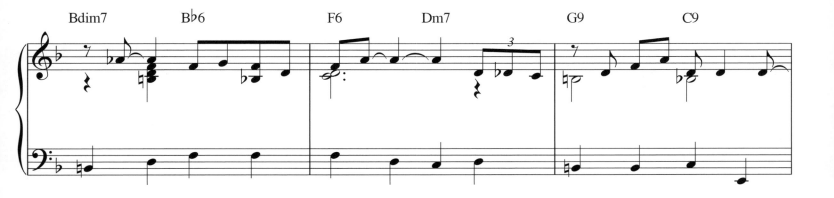

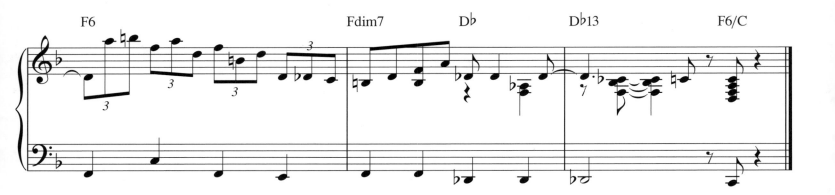

SOMETIMES I'M HAPPY

Words by CLIFFORD GREY and IRVING CAESAR
Music by VINCENT YOUMANS

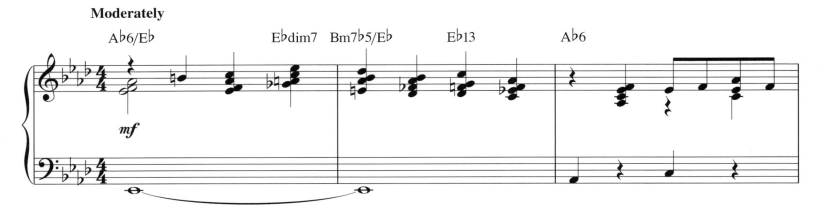

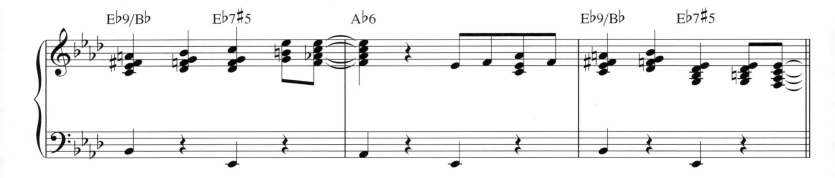

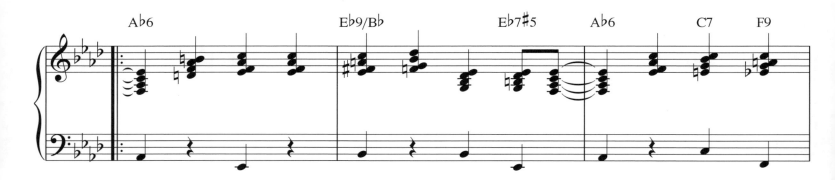

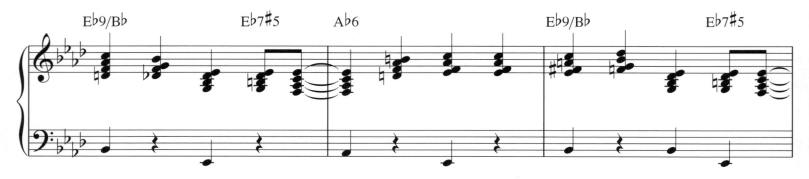

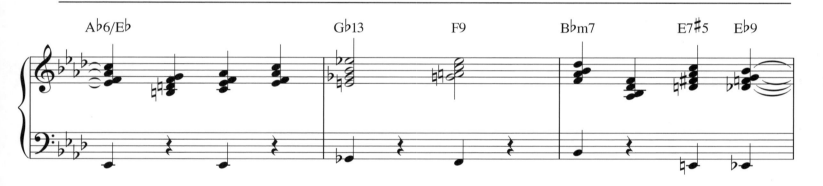

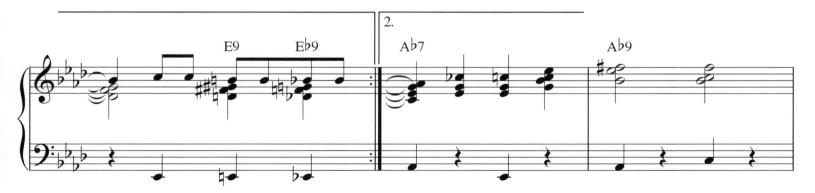

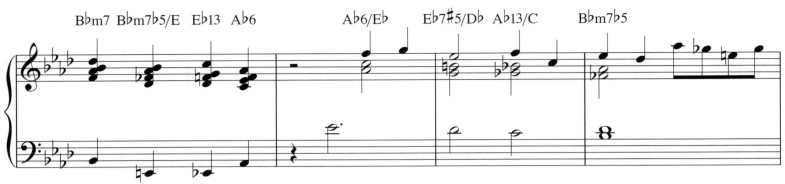

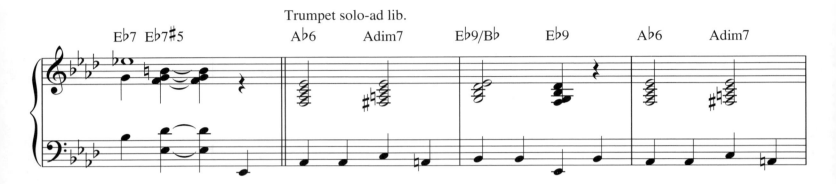

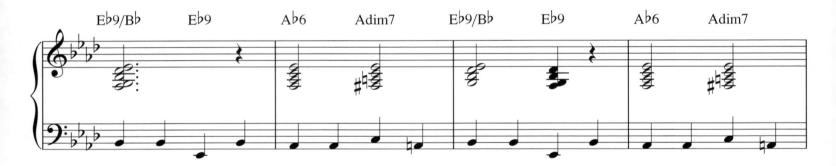

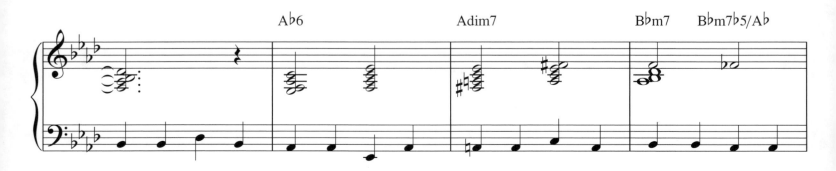

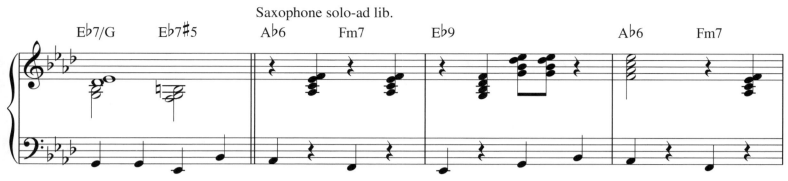

Saxophone solo-ad lib.

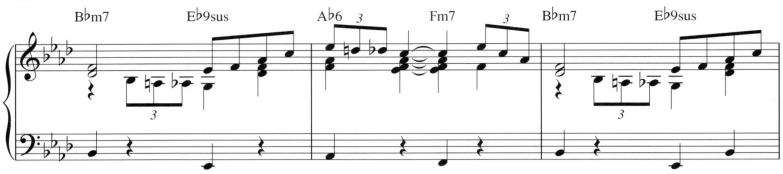

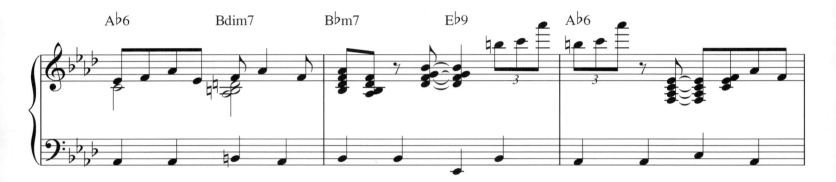

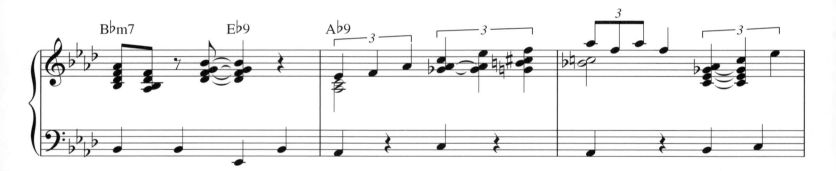

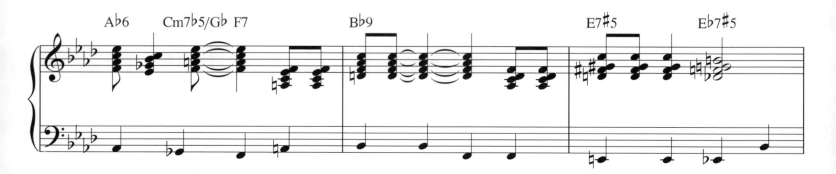

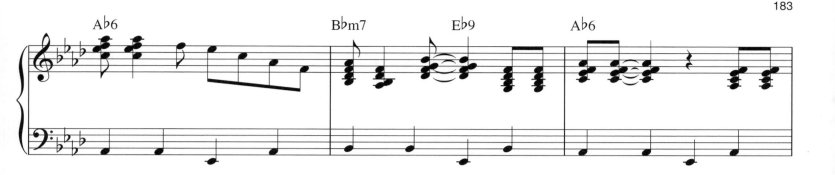

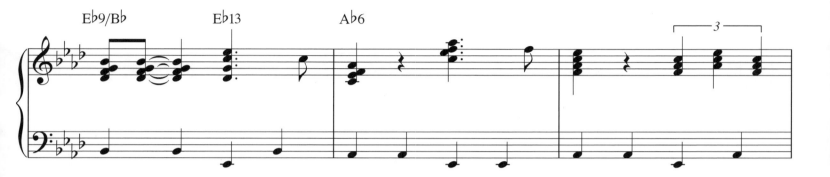

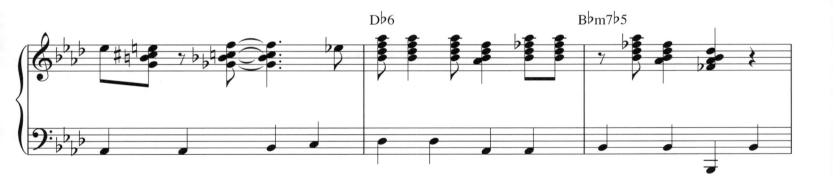

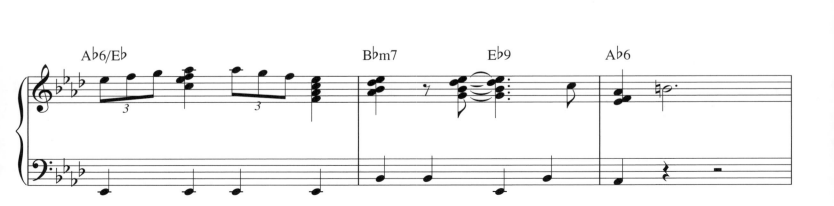

Benny Goodman clarinet solo:

SUGAR FOOT STOMP

Lyric by WALTER MELROSE
Music by JOE OLIVER

Moderately bright Swing

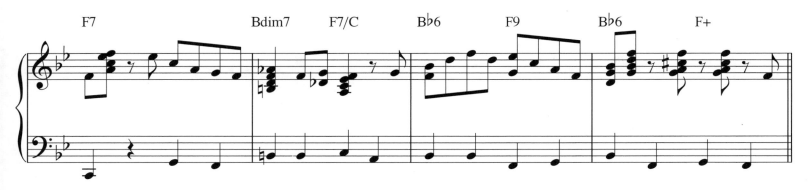

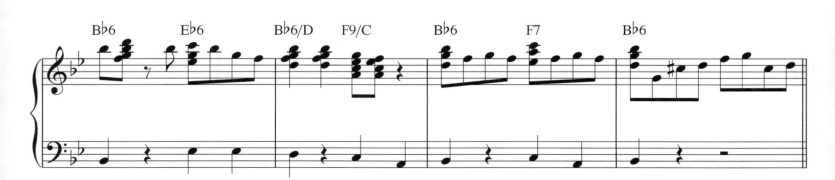

Trumpet solo:

Stop time

Eb7   Bb6

F7   F7#5   Bb

Bb6   Bb13

Stop time

Eb6   Cm7b5   Bb6

Benny Goodman clarinet solo:

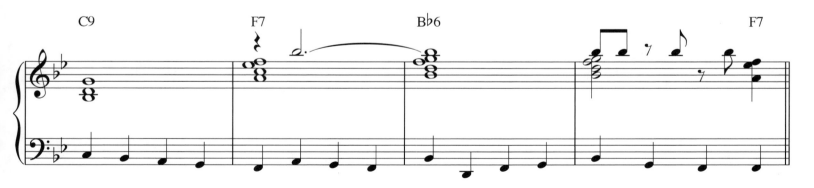

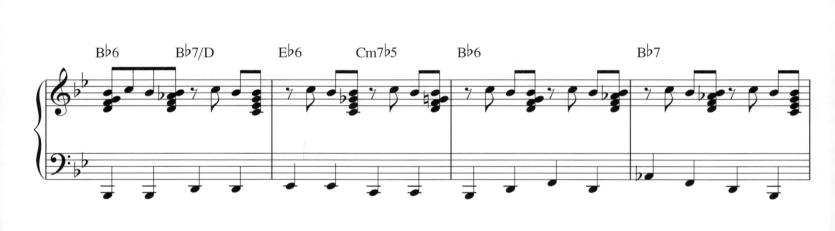

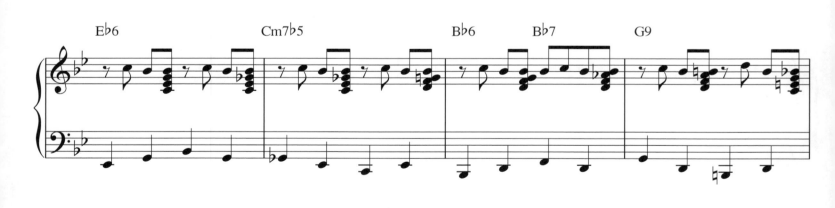

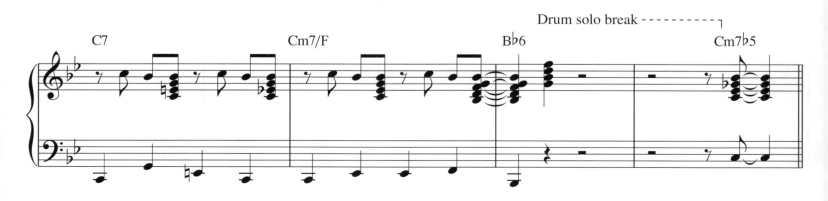

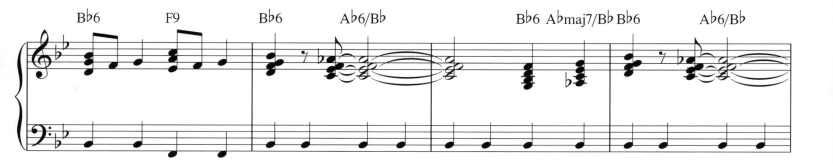

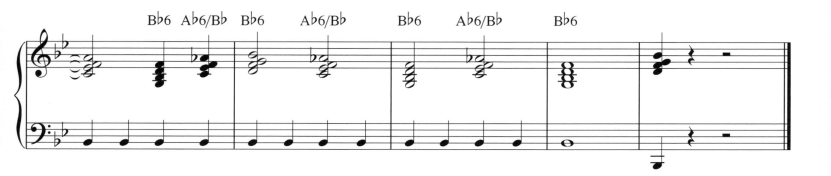

STEALIN' APPLES

Words by ANDY RAZAF
Music by THOMAS "FATS" WALLER

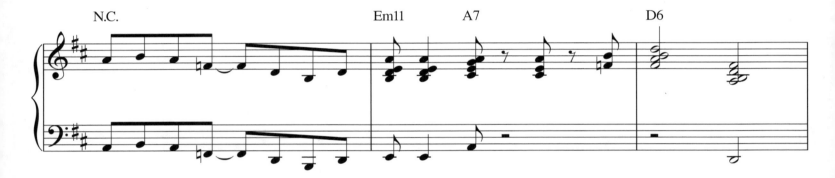

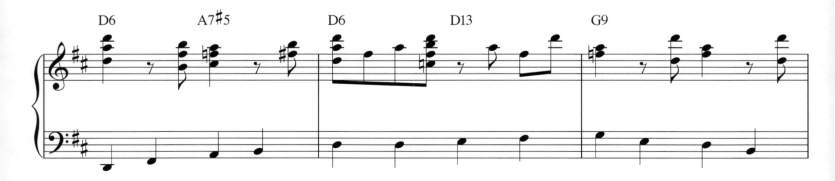

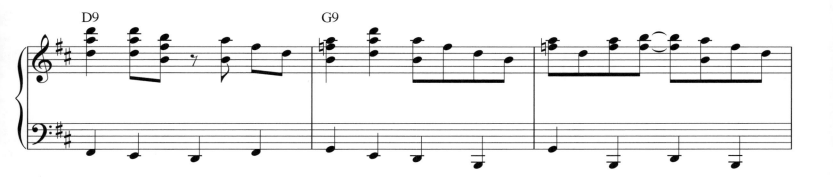

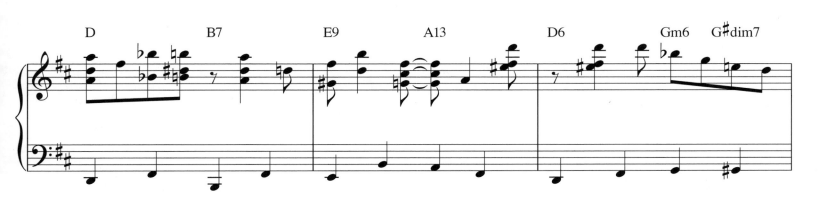

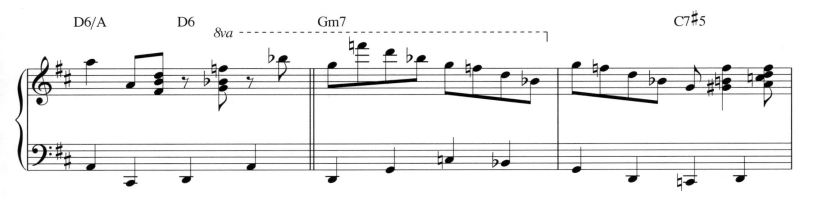

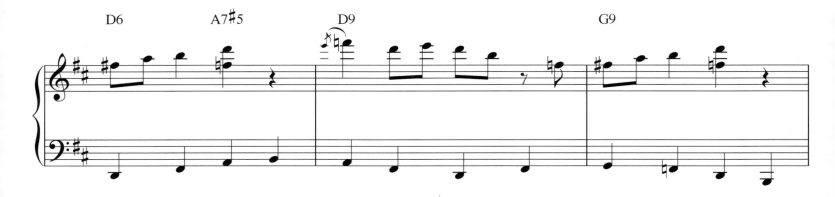

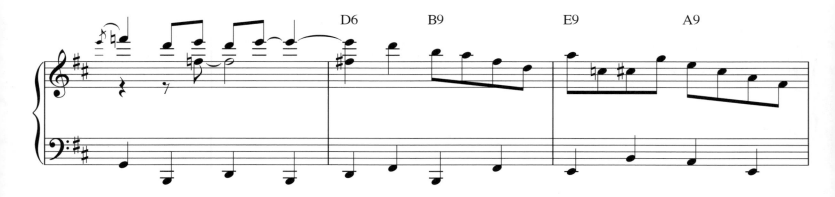

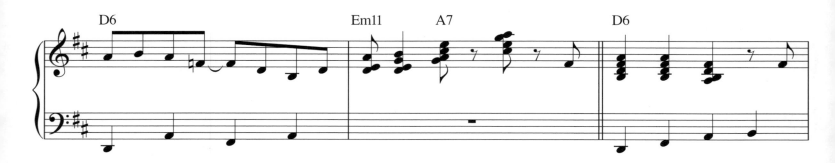

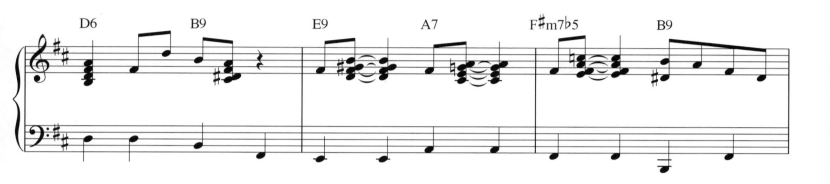

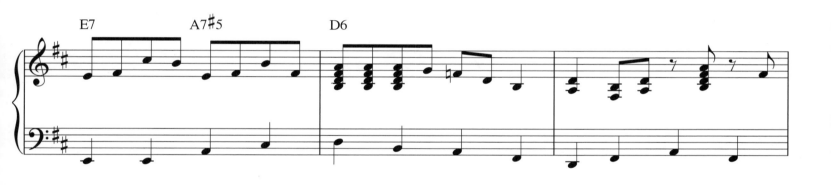

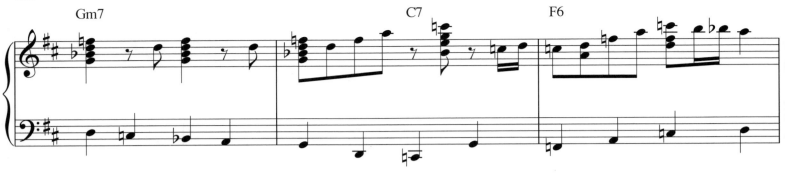

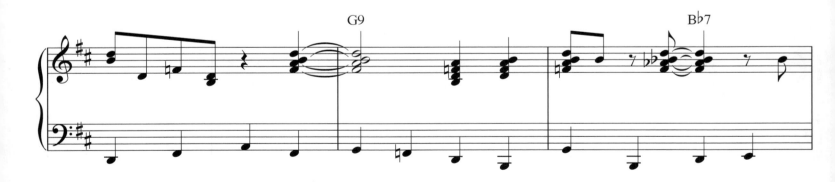

Trumpet solo-ad lib.

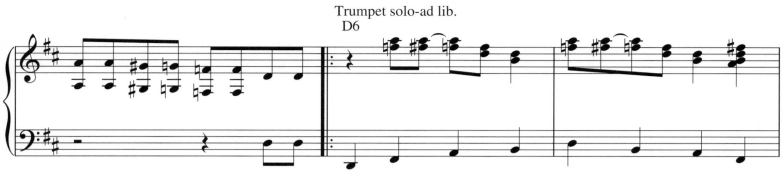

Clarinet solo-ad lib.

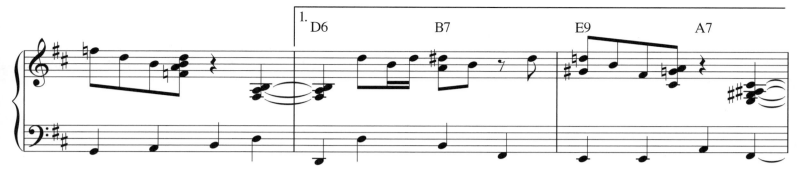

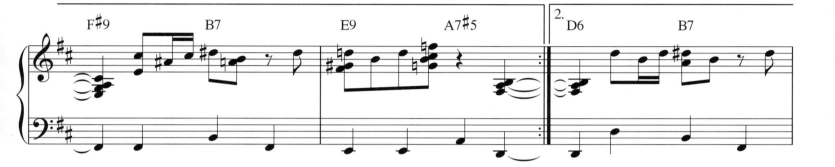

Benny Goodman clarinet solo:

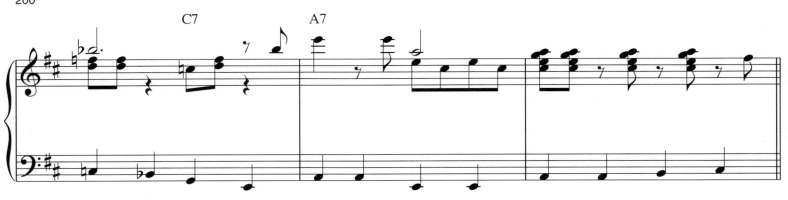

Clarinet solo-ad lib.
Tutti:

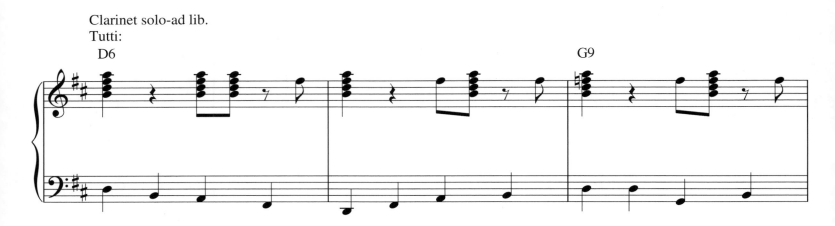

WHY DON'T YOU DO RIGHT
(GET ME SOME MONEY, TOO!)

By JOE McCOY

Moderate Swing

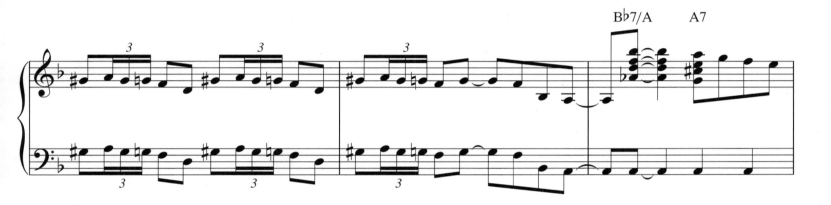

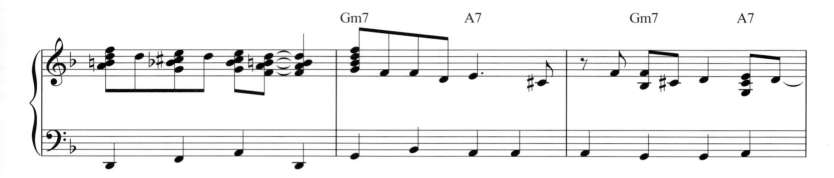

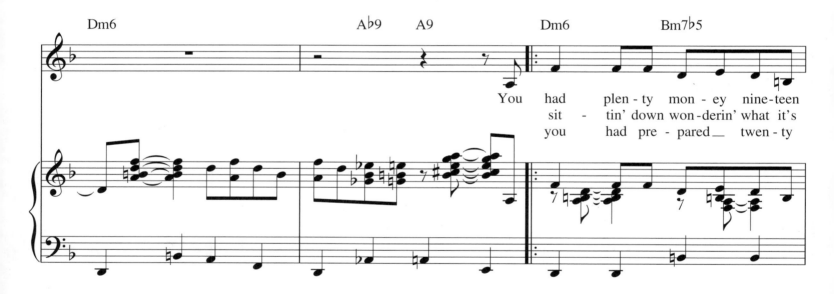

You had plen - ty mon - ey nine - teen
sit - tin' down won - derin' what it's
you had pre - pared __ twen - ty

twen - ty two. __ You let oth - er wom - en make a
all a - bout. __ You ain't got no mon - ey; they will
years a - go __ you would - n't be wan - derin' now from

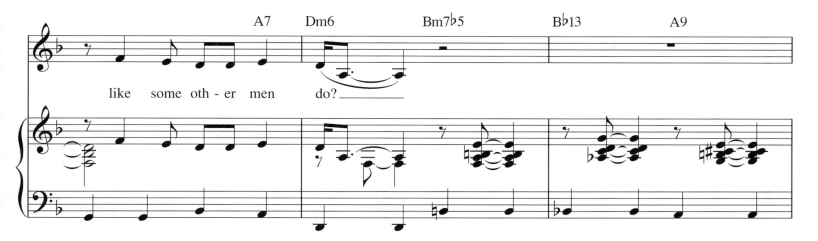

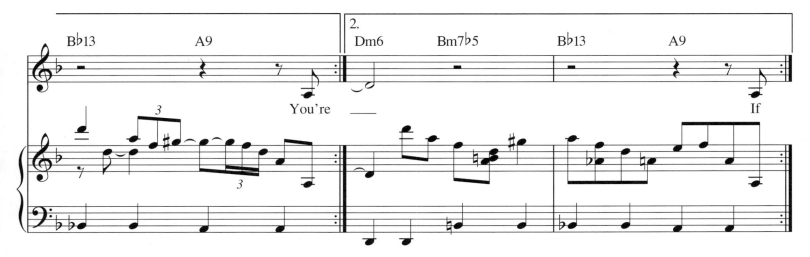

204

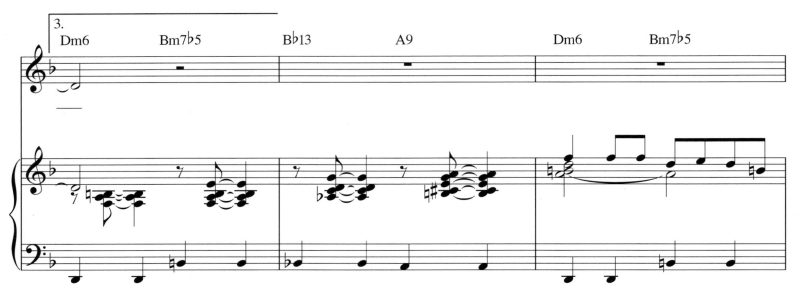

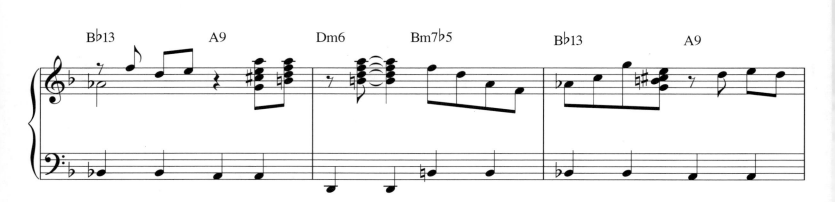

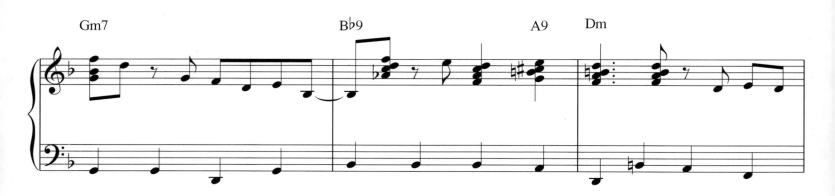

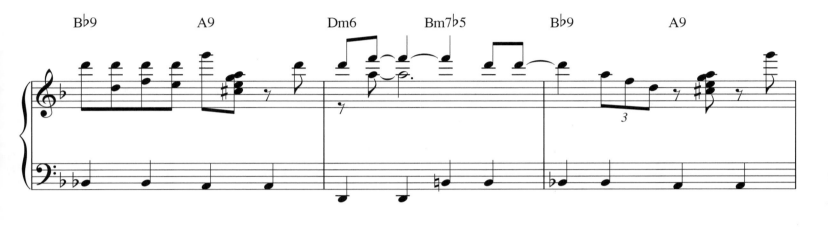

206

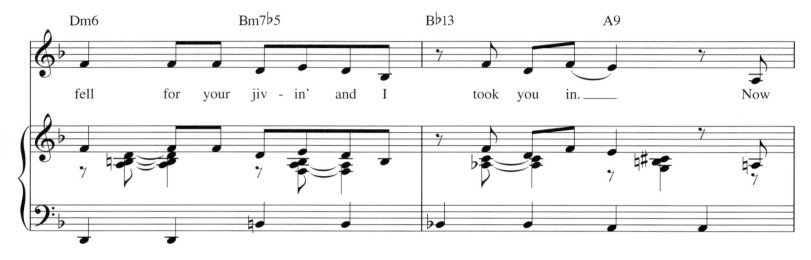

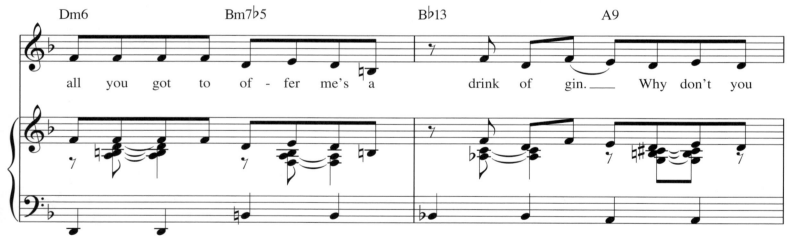

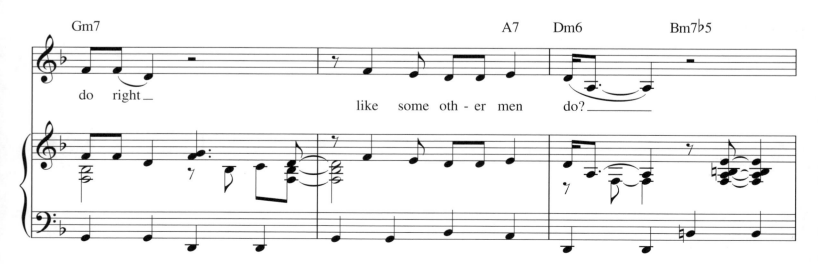

207

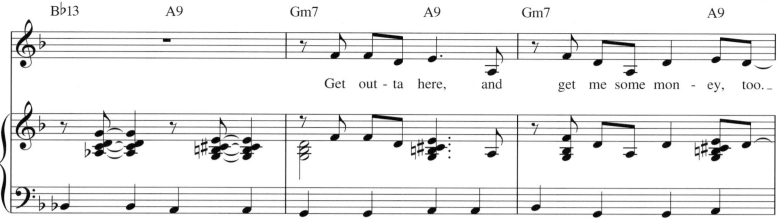

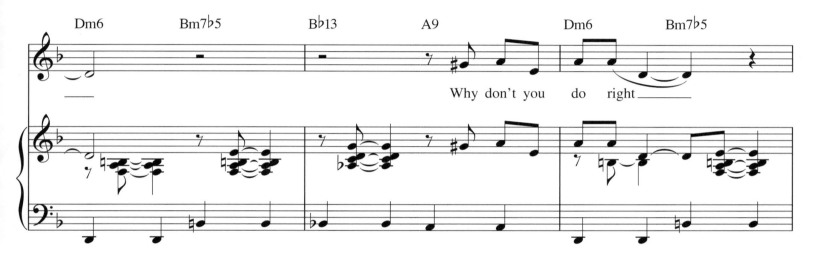

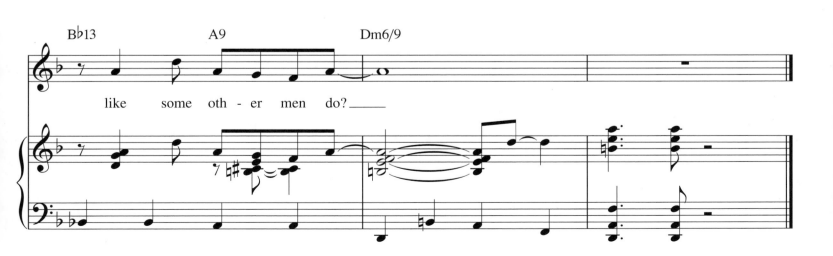

THE WORLD IS WAITING FOR THE SUNRISE

Words by EUGENE LOCKHART
Music by ERNEST SEITZ

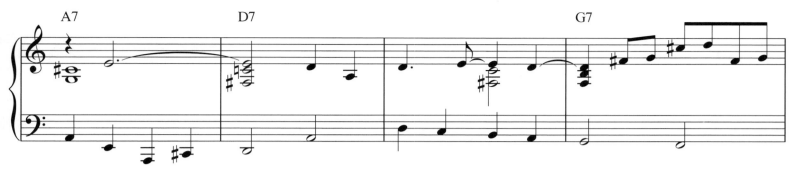

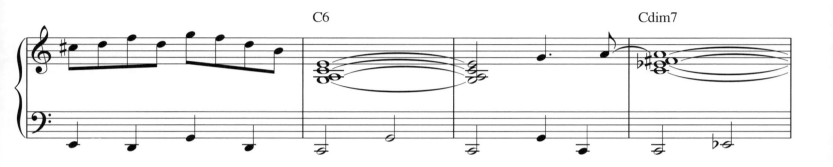

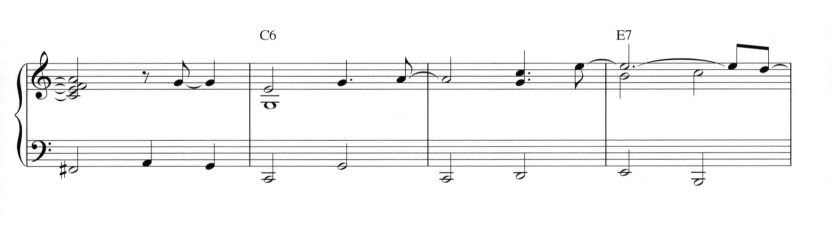

Piano solo:

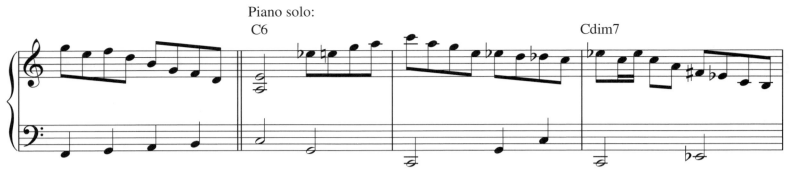

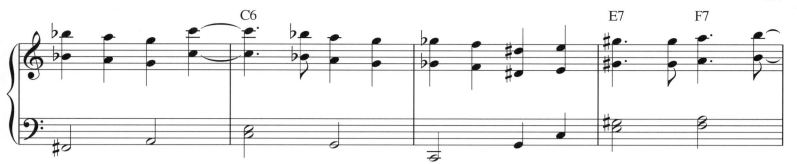

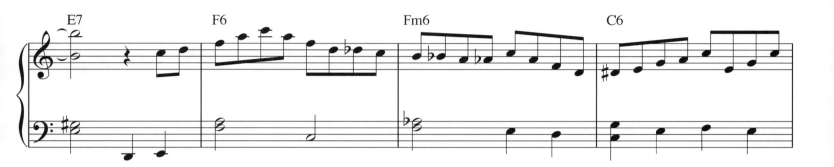

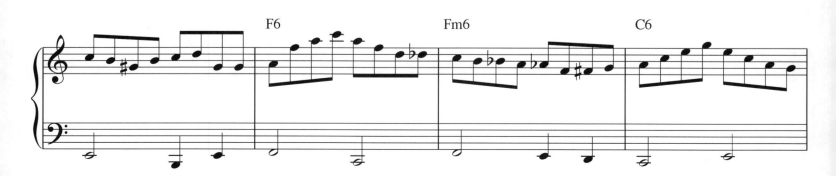

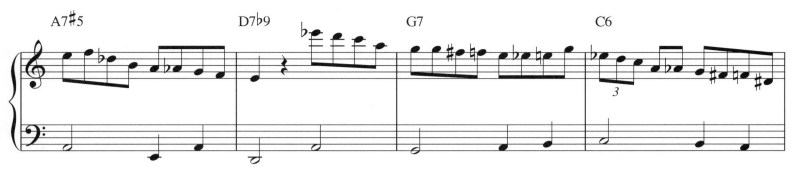

Benny Goodman clarinet solo:

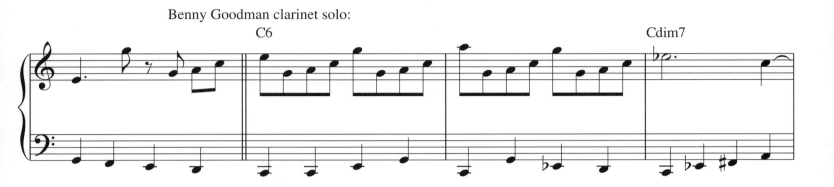

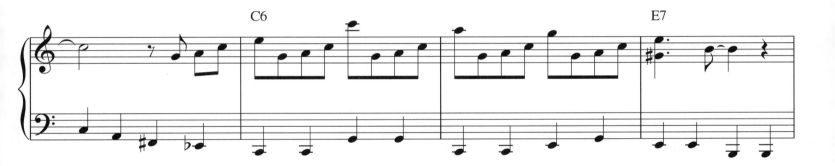

214

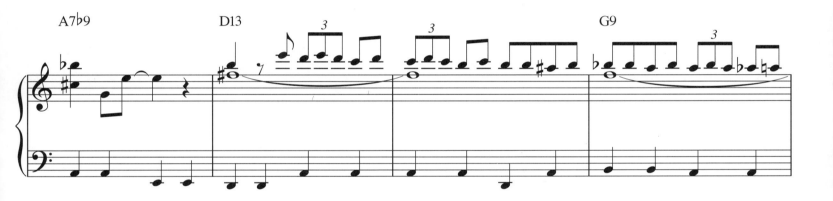

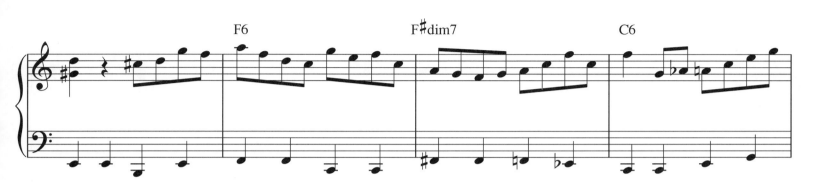

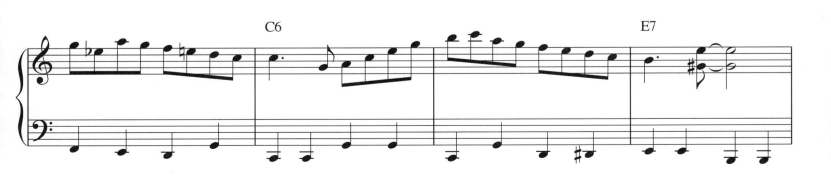

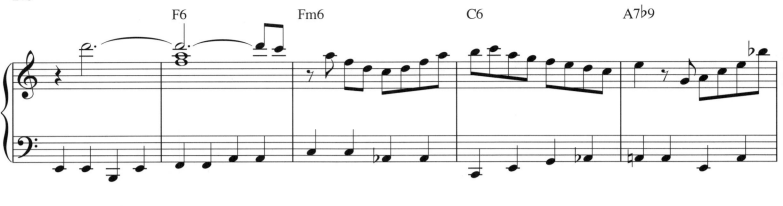

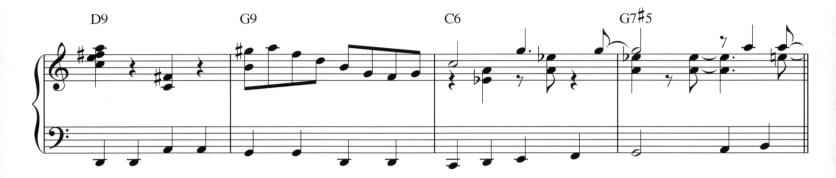

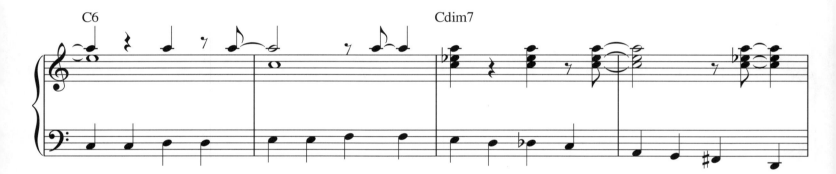

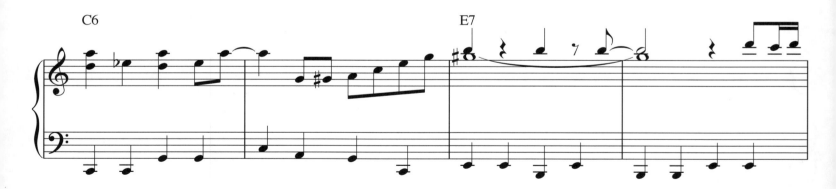

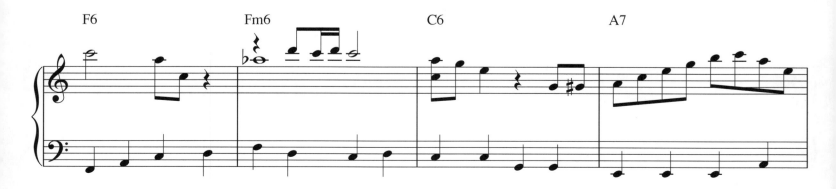

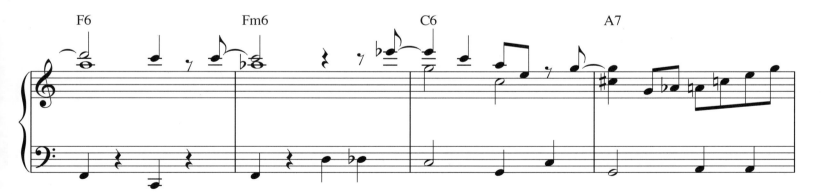

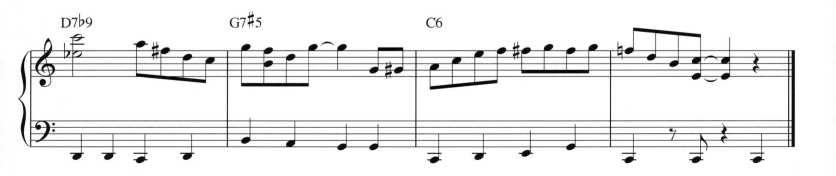

THIS YEAR'S KISSES

from the 20th Century Fox Motion Picture ON THE AVENUE

Words and Music by
IRVING BERLIN

Moderate Two-Beat Swing

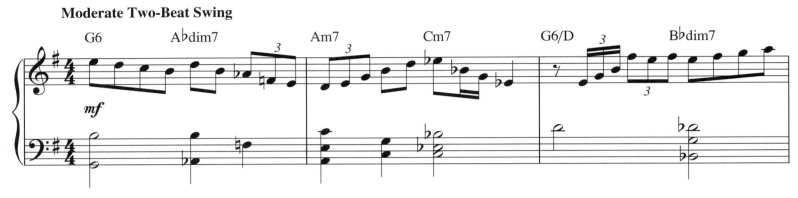

Saxophone solo:

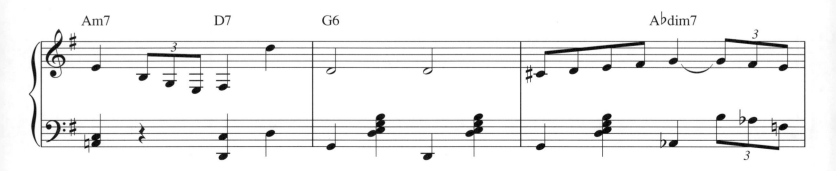

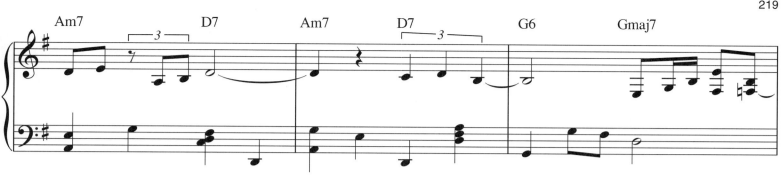

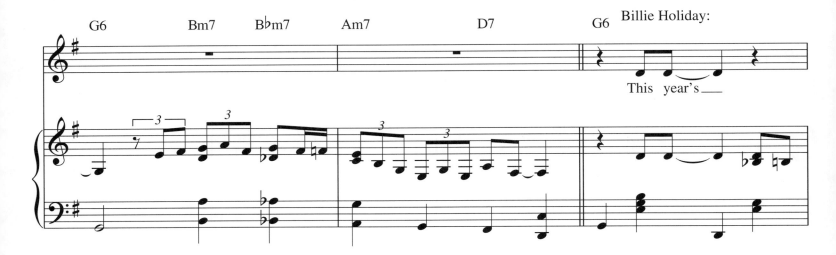

Billie Holiday:

This year's___

crop of ___ kiss - es ___ don't seem ___ as ___ sweet to

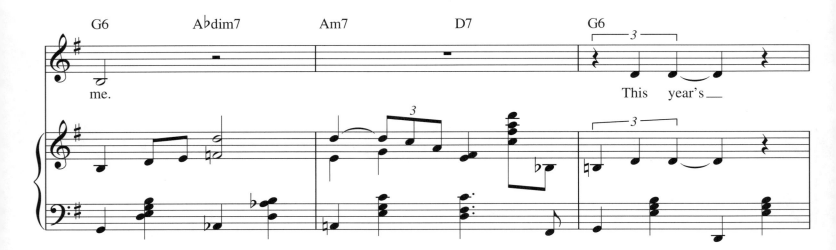

me.

This year's___

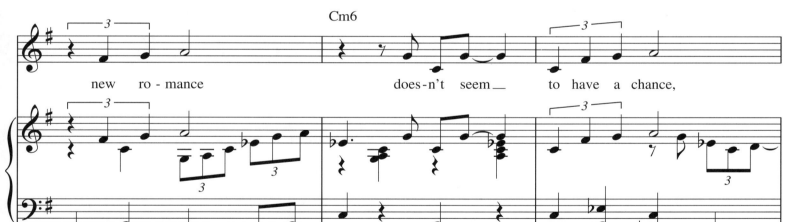

This year's ___ crop of ___ kiss - es ___

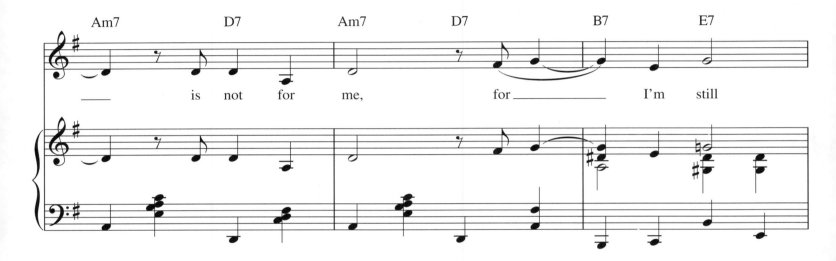

___ is not for me, for ___ I'm still

wear - in' last ___ year's ___ love. ___

Piano solo:

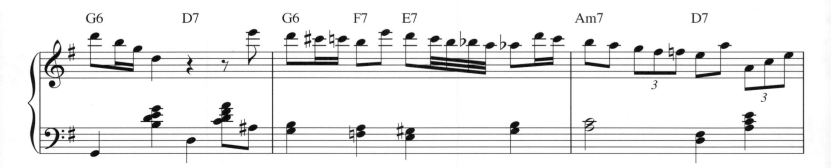

223

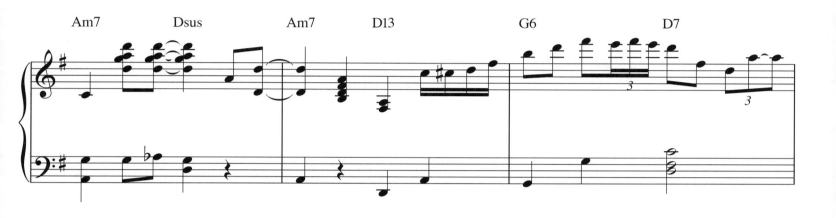

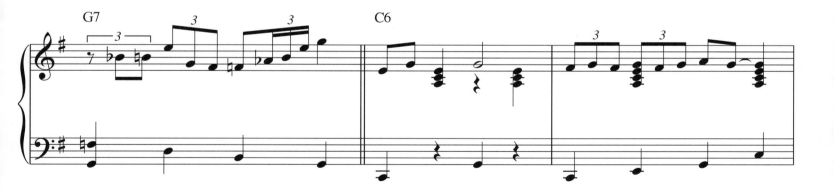

224

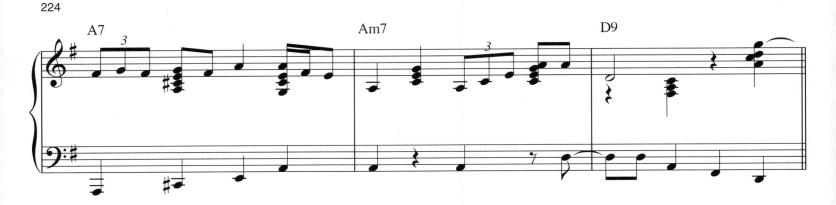

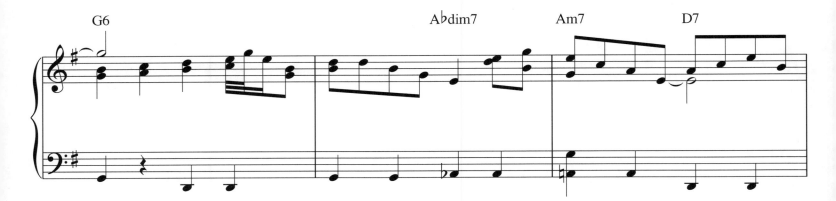

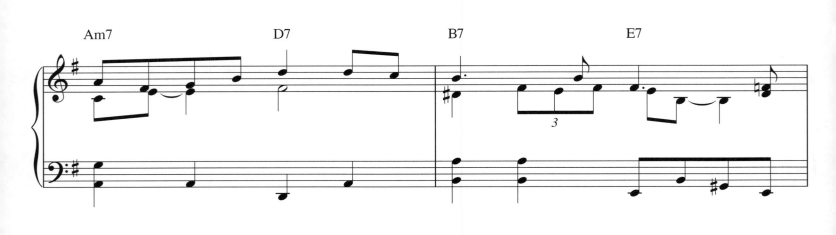

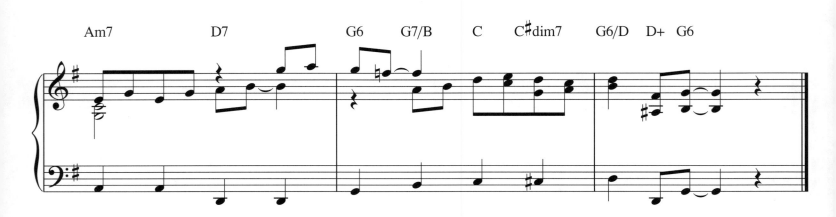